Golf is a game of expletives not deleted.
—Dr. Irving A. Gladstone

THE QU⦿TABLE
GOLFER

THE GREATEST THINGS EVER SAID ABOUT
THE GREATEST @*!!?#! GAME EVER PLAYED

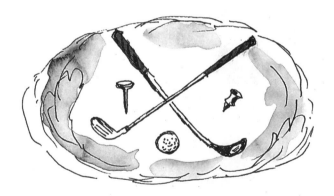

Robert Windeler
Illustrated by Allan Drummond

RUNNING PRESS
PHILADELPHIA · LONDON

FOR CHARLES F. (CHUCK) MITCHELL,
WHOSE PATIENCE, DEDICATION, AND DETERMINATION
MAKE HIM AN EVEN BETTER FRIEND
THAN HE IS A GOLFER.

© 1998 by Robert Windeler
Cover and interior illustrations © Allan Drummond

All rights reserved under the Pan-American and International Copyright Conventions

Printed in the United States of America

This book may not be reproduced in whole or in part, in any form or by any means,
electronic or mechanical, including photocopying, recording, or by any information storage
and retrieval system now known or hereafter invented, without written permission from the publisher.

9   8   7   6   5   4   3   2   1
Digit on the right indicates the number of this printing

Library of Congress Cataloging-in-Publication Number 97-66820

ISBN 0-7624-0269-5

Cover and interior design by Corinda Cook

This book may be ordered by mail from the publisher.
Please include $2.50 for postage and handling. *But try your bookstore first!*

Running Press Book Publishers
125 South Twenty-second Street
Philadelphia, Pennsylvania 19103-4399

ACKNOWLEDGEMENTS

A relative of mine I never knew, George Herbert Windeler, did as much as any other Englishman to establish the game of golf in America around a hundred years ago. A tireless organizer of The Country Club of Brookline, Massachusetts, he was President of the United States Golf Association in the watershed year of 1903, when the rubber-cored Haskell ball achieved universal acceptance and changed the playing of golf forever. I like to think that G. H. W.'s irrepressible spirit, and that of his daughter, Evelyn Windeler Robertson, whom I knew very well indeed, have somehow guided me in this survey of several centuries' worth of words on golf.

My maternal grandfather, Frederick W. DeVoe, took me to my first golf course (and also my first movie) when I was five years old. I was as much struck by the outdoor ambiance as I was by the indoor one—though it took me longer to get around to writing about golf than it did the movies. The late William H. Davis, who founded *Golf Digest* and later sold it to the New York Times Company, was the first person to believe that I could write about golf in the same way as I wrote about entertainment, and that there was no reason why I couldn't do both. Thanks to Bill, who also took me to my first British Open, I began doing just that. (It helped that my first work for *Golf Digest* was a review of the movie *Caddyshack*).

The Los Angeles Country Club, with its rich one hundred years of history and its many unforgettable characters, was the ideal place for me to wallow in the whole story of golf and golfers, for the better part of two years. The gorgeously produced result of that effort, the centennial history *Links With a Past*, certainly gave me a big head start on the present volume. I'm grateful to the board and membership of L.A.C.C., and especially to the club's longtime general manager, Jim Brewer, for his unflagging enthusiasm for and support of the project. His assistants, Steve Wilson and Elizabeth Carey, were also unfailingly helpful and encouraging.

Brendan Cahill of Running Press may have found me through the World Wide Web, but he quickly emerged as a flesh-and-blood human being whose caring determination gives me hope for the new generation of book editors.

The unquestioned godmothers of *The Quotable Golfer* are Saundra Sheffer and Marge Dewey, the doyennes of the remarkable and undersung Ralph W. Miller Golf Library in Industry Hills, California. Saundra, who also edited *Links With a Past*, and Marge, the Miller's head librarian, not only provided the initial link between Brendan and me, they also provided a congenial and encyclopedic home for my initial research, and much-needed and appreciated biographical help at the end.

THE COURSE

FRONT NINE

BACK NINE (AND THEN SOME)

CHAPTER ONE

THE GREATEST GAME

Golf is more exacting than racing, cards, speculation or matrimony.

In almost all other games you pit yourself against a moral foe;

in golf it is yourself against the world: no human being stays your

progress as you drive your ball over the face of the globe.

—Arnold Haultain

Almost no one is neutral about what Bobby Jones called "The Greatest Game." Golf becomes a life-long obsession for some, and represents total tedium to others. Great or not, golf is a *game*—requiring finesse, inner strength and strategy—rather than a sport—relying on a particular physiology, brute strength, or motor skills. Some 25 million (and counting) Americans play golf regularly, and at least that many more golfers live in the rest of the world, with the greatest concentrations in Great Britain and Ireland, Germany, Japan, South Africa, and Australia. Although golf has been "the sport of princes" for five hundred years, golf always attracted players from other strata of society. And the current quantum growth in the popularity of the game has occurred equally among elitist circles and inner-city youth. The only limitations are the costs of course fees and equipment—Americans spend $2 billion a year on the latter.

Today's golfer can be any age, of either sex, fat or thin, tall or short, even drunk or sober. No amount of aerobic or other exercise will make him or her a better golfer. And no amount of golf will provide him or her any exercise at all— apart from the almost extinct act of walking to the next hole rather than riding in a golf cart. In fact, the greatest distinction between golf and other games is the vast amount of time each player has to stand around and think about what to do next.

While tournament golf and even casual Sunday foursomes can be highly competitive, a golfer needs no opponent other than the course he or she is playing, and his or her own previous or average score. The objective of the game—to hit a ball into each of eighteen (or nine, or thirty-six) holes on a course—is so basic that golf is self-governing, without the need for referees or umpires. Even the origin of the name is simple: "golf" comes from *kolbe,* the Dutch word for club. Yet, for all its seeming simplicity, golf becomes more difficult and puzzling the more it is studied. And it is studied, analyzed, written, and read about far more than any other game.

Willie Nelson, the great singer/songwriter who built his own private golf course, once said that there were "some golf shots I wouldn't trade for an orgasm."

Like most fanaticisms, golf is only truly understood by its fanatics.

Golf is deceptively simple, endlessly complicated. A child can play it well, and a grown man can never master it. Any single round of it is full of unexpected triumphs and seemingly perfect shots that end in disaster. It is almost a science, yet it is a puzzle without an answer. It is gratifying and tantalizing, precise and unpredictable. It requires complete concentration and total relaxation. It satisfies the soul and frustrates the intellect. It is at the same time rewarding and maddening—and it is without doubt the greatest game mankind has ever invented.

—Robert Forgan

Unlike the other Scotch game of whiskey drinking, excess in it is not injurious to your health.

—Sir Walter Simpson

The determining bulk of Scotch people had heard of golf ever since they had heard of God; and often considered the two as of equal importance.

—G. K. Chesterton

In so many English sports, something flying or running has to be killed or injured; golf calls for no drop of blood from any living creature.

—Henry Leach

The soldier, having sought the bubble reputation in the cannon's mouth,
may earn laurels on a field which shall be bloodless and receive
at least a purer pleasure from deftly landing his ball in the hole than ever
came to him from letting daylight into his fellow mortals.

—Dr. Proudfoot

Golf is a non-violent game, played violently from within.

—Bob Toski

On the golf course, a man may be the dogged victim of inexorable fate,
be struck down by an appalling stroke of tragedy, become the hero
of unbelievable melodrama, or the clown in a side-splitting
comedy—Any of these within a few hours, and all without having
to bury a corpse or repair a tangled personality.

—Bobby Jones

I guess there is nothing that will get your mind off everything like golf.
I have never been depressed enough to take up the game but
they say you get so sore at yourself you forget to hate your enemies.

—Will Rogers

The glorious thing is that thousands of golfers, in park land,
on windy downs, in gorse, in heather, by the many-sounding seas,
enjoy their imbecilities, revel in their infirmities, and from
failure itself draw that final victory—the triumph of hope.

—R. C. Robertson-Glasgow

WHAT IS THIS THING CALLED GOLF?

Charles (Chick) Evans was the first player to win the American Amateur championship and U.S. Open championship in the same year, triumphing at the Open with a score of 286 (a record that stood for two decades), while using a set of only seven hickory-shafted clubs.

In 1929, Evans, who never turned pro, attempted to explain the golf phenomenon that was then sweeping the nation to New York book magnate M. Lincoln Schuster, of the publishing company Simon & Schuster.

Evans began by saying, "It's a game."

"Is it?" Schuster replied. "I was beginning to think it was a religion, or a health-cure, or a business."

**Golf recapitulates evolution.
It is a microcosm of the world,
a projection of all our hopes and fears.**
—Adam Greene

Golf is an awkward set of bodily contortions
designed to produce a graceful result.
—Tommy Armour

Golf is life. If you can't take golf, you can't take life.
—American proverb

Golf is the hardest sport. . . . One day you're up on cloud nine
and the next day you couldn't scratch a whale's belly.
—Sam Snead

Golf is a humbling game.
—George Low, Sr.

Golf makes liars out of honest men, cheats out of altruists,
cowards out of brave men, and fools out of everybody.
—Milton Gross

Golf puts a man's character on the anvil
and his richest qualities—patience, poise, restraint—to the flame.
—Billy Casper

Golf is like a grindstone: whether it grinds you down
or polishes you up depends on what you're made of.
—English saying

**It is a test of temper, a trial of honor,
a revealer of character. It means going into God's
out of doors, getting close to nature, fresh air
and exercise, a sweeping of mental cobwebs
and a genuine relaxation of tired tissues.**
—David Forgan

Like one's own children, golf has an uncanny way of endearing
itself to us while at the same time evoking every weakness
of mind and character, no matter how well hidden.
—W. Timothy Gallwey

Golf may be played on Sunday, not being a game
within the view of the law, but being a form of moral effort.
—Stephen Butler Leacock

If you watch a game, it's fun.
If you play at it, it's recreation.
If you work at it, it's golf.
—Bob Hope

Golf is a way of testing ourselves while enjoying ourselves.
—Arnold Palmer

Beyond the fact that it is a limitless arena for the full play of human nature,
there is no sure accounting for golf's fascination. Obviously yet
mysteriously, it furnishes its devotees with an intense, many-sided, and abiding
pleasure unlike that which any other form of recreation affords. . . . Perhaps
it is nothing more than the best game man has ever devised.
—Herbert Warren Wind

Golf is an artist's game, its palette full of dewy grass
and azure sky and well-raked bunkers. It is a philosopher's game,
engaging wind and water to play strategic tricks on our concentration.
And it is a gambler's game, asking us whether is will be the nerve
to aim for the flagstick or the caution to settle for a probable bogey.
—Reg Murphy

[Golf] is visual: it has texture, it has emotion; it has power.
—Betty Jameson

Golf is a game with the soul of a 1956 Rotarian.
—Bill Mandel

After you get the basics down, it's all mental.
—Ken Venturi

Excessive golfing dwarfs the intellect. Nor is this to be wondered at when we consider that the more fatuously vacant the mind is, the better for play. It has been observed that absolute idiots play the steadiest.
—Sir Walter Simpson

The game of golf is ninety percent mental and ten percent mental.
—Mulligan's Laws

Let's face it, ninety-five percent of this game is mental.
A guy plays lousy golf he doesn't need a pro, he needs a shrink.
—Tom Murphy

Golf has robbed old age of its regrets,
for it can be played from the cradle to the grave.
—Gustav Kobbé

Golf, like measles, should be caught young, for,
if postponed to riper years, the results may be serious.
—P. G. Wodehouse

When you fall in love with golf,
you seldom fall easy: it's obsession at first sight.
—Thomas Boswell

A hundred years of experience has demonstrated
that the game is temporary insanity practiced in a cow pasture.
—Dave Kindred

Golf is a science, the study of a lifetime,
in which you can exhaust yourself but never your subject.
—David Forgan

CHAPTER TWO

GOLF THROUGH THE AGES

When that pre-historic Dutchman . . . carried his kolb *or club over to Leith*

in a smack, deep-laden with ankers of Schiedam, he little dreamt that he was draining

the life blood of his land and sprinkling its life-giving drops over the links of North

Britain. The wildest dreams never forecast the numbers or the prowess

of the stalwart men and lissome girls who now honor that Dutchman's memory and

drive the wild eccentric guttie afar over the shining reaches by the sea.

—W. F. Collier

T he Dutch began playing a golf-like game in the North Holland province of the Low Countries, in what is now Belgium and the Netherlands, perhaps as early as 1297—although in *colf* or *colven*, as it was called, the ball was aimed at above-ground targets. The earliest known written references to golf—in Dutch and English—were prohibitions. The first surviving golf quote imposed a stiff fine for playing the game. In 1360, the Southern Netherlands Ordinance Book of Brussells declared: *"Item wie met colven tsolt es om twintich scell' oft op hare overste cleet."* ("Whoever plays ball with a club, that is at twenty shillings or at their upper garment," literally the shirt off his—presumably—back, a common punishment in the fourteenth century.)

Around 1450, Scotland, determined to maintain its independence from England, traded with Holland almost exclusively. Dutch merchants exported wooden clubs and feather balls along with more prosaic items to Scotland. From within the Scottish population arose an ardent army of golfers. Three kings in a row condemned the game in the belief that golf seduced the citizen militiamen away from archery practice at a time when skilled archers were needed to defend against the frequent English invasions. The Scottish golfing population ignored royal bans on their game. James IV eventually bowed to the inevitable and rescinded the rule. He even became a golfer himself. When he married a daughter of King Henry VII, James IV introduced golf into England, and the world has never been the same since.

Golf was introduced into the United States just before the Revolution by Scottish artisans, particularly printers. Benjamin Rush, a signer of the Declaration of Independence, wrote the first book in America to mention golf, *Sermons to Gentlemen Upon Temperence and Exercise.* He extolled the virtues of the game, claiming that "a man would live ten years longer for this exercise once or twice a week."

But it would be another 120 years before the game really took hold in America. Then, in the 1890s, literally hundreds of golf courses sprang up, from Brookline, Massachusetts and Shinnecock Hills, Long Island in the East, to Los Angeles and Phoenix in the West. Sometimes the courses were on not entirely converted farmland. Early critics referred to golf as "cow-pasture pool."

The growth of automobile ownership and the proliferation of professional tournaments, along with the visibility of celebrity players such as silent movie stars, inspired a surge in golf's popularity. In the 1950s, television and a highly visible, popular golfing president, Dwight Eisenhower, led a second major spurt in the growth of the game, which was now spreading across the globe. Today the game is played on 15,700 public and private courses in the United States alone, and golf has taken yet another quantum leap thanks to cable television, corporate sponsorship of professional tournaments, aggressive marketing of new equipment, and dynamic young players such as Tiger Woods.

Ever since golf began—Scottish historians have settled on the year
1100 as a reasonable date of birth—the game has been an enigma.
—Herbert Warren Wind

Unlike many sports, golf does not enjoy the privilege of knowing its exact birthright.
—Ian Morrison

Golf is a game with a shady past. Its actual birth is shrouded in mystery.
No one is quite certain when or where it drew its first tortured breath.
Historians only know that the first anguished squalls of the infant came
rolling over the moors of Scotland in the fifteenth century.
Golf cannot point to a legal father, such as baseball in the case of Abner
Doubleday or basketball in the case of Dr. James A. Naismith.
In fact, there is a question that golf was ever born at all. As some scientists
contend in regard to man himself, the game may have just evolved.
—Will Grimsley

The Scots say that Nature itself dictated that golf should be played
by the seashore. Rather, the Scots saw in the eroded seacoasts
a cheap battleground on which they could whip their fellow men
in a game based on the Calvinist doctrine that man is meant to suffer
here below and never more than when he goes out to enjoy himself.
—Alistair Cooke

Nobody strikes the ball on the streets with clubs with lead or iron heads.

—Ordinance of Zierikzee (Netherlands), 1429

It is decreeted and ordained . . . that the Fute-ball and Golfe
be utterly cryed downe, and not to be used. And as tuitching the Fute-ball
and the Golfe, to be punished by the Barronniss un-law.

—James II of Scotland, 1457

The ball people with their balls shall post themselves along
the canal from the bridge in front of Master Arent Goes.

—Magistrates of Bergen op Zoom (Netherlands), 1461

Fute-ball and Golfe be abused in time cumming,
and that the buttes be made up, and schuting used.

—James III of Scotland, 1471

It is statute and ordained that in na place of the Realme there be used Fute-ball, Golfe or uther sik unproffitable sportes.

—James IV of Scotland, 1491

Ye will remember to bring with you ane dossen of commoun golf ballis to me and David Moncrieff.

—Letter from the Orkney Islands, Scotland, 1585

Dyvers inhabitants of the burgh repairs upon the Sabboth day
to the town of Leith, and in tyme of sermons ae sene vagrant about the
streets, drynking in taverns, or otherwayes at golf, aicherie, or other
pastymes, uponn the linkes, thairby profaning the Sabboth day.

—Edinburgh Council, 1593

Walter Hay, goldsmith, accusit for playing at the boulis and golf upoun Sundaye in the tyme of the sermon.

—Records of Elgin, 1596

About this toun are the fairest and largest linkes of any pairt of Scotland,
fitt for Archery, Goffing, Ryding, and all other exercises;
they doe surpasse the feilds of Montrose or St. Andrews.

—Sir Robert Gordon, describing Dornoch, 1630

ROYAL AND ANCIENT

With six sovereign monarchs of the House of Stuart avid players, golf rightly became known as the "Royal and Ancient Game." Catherine of Aragon, the first wife of Henry VIII, wrote of her involvement with "the golf" while her husband was off hunting or otherwise engaged. Playing the game probably prolonged Catherine's marriage to Henry and made him the first prominent golf widower. His cousin, Mary Queen of Scots, was so keen on the game that she was seen driving on the Links of Leith only three days after the murder of her husband, Lord Darnley, in 1567. Her heir, James VI of Scotland (who became James I of England following the death of Elizabeth I) appointed the first royal clubmaker in 1603, and the first royal ball-maker in 1618.

James VI's son Henry, Prince of Wales, was known throughout the kingdom for the quality of his drives, and his successor, Charles I, reportedly interrupted his round of golf with great reluctance when word of the Irish Rebellion was brought to him on the Links of Leith in 1642. More than forty years later, Leith was the grounds for another historical battle—the first-ever international foursome match, between England and Scotland.

Here one makes clubs fine and noble.
Play colf with pleasure, not brawls.
Play for a pint or a gallon.
Let the winter be cold and hard.
We play the ball just the same.
—Sign on a house in Haarlem, Holland, 1650

**Tennis is not in use amongst us, but in lieu
of that, you have that excellent recreation of goff-ball
than which truly I do not know better.**
—The Marquis of Argyll, 1661

Of this diversion the Scots are so fond, that, when the weather will permit,
you may see a multitude of all ranks, from the senator
of justice to the lowest tradesman, mingled together, in their shirts,
and following the balls with utmost eagerness.
—Tobias Smollett, 1771

May your balls, as they fly and whiz through the air
Knock down the blue devils, dull sorrow and care
May your health be preserved, with strength active and bold
Long traverse the green, and forget to grow old.
—Henry Callender, Royal Blackheath Club secretary and captain in 1790, 1801, and 1807

Gof is an exercise which is much used by the Gentlemen of Scotland.
A large common in which there are several little holes is chosen for the purpose.
It is played with little leather balls stuffed with feathers;
and sticks made somewhat in the form of a handy-wicket. He who puts a ball
into a given number of holes, with the fewest strokes, gets the game.
—Benjamin Rush, signer of the *Declaration of Independence*

Long driving, if it be not the most deadly, is certainly the most dashing
and fascinating part of the game; and of all others the principal difficulty
of the Golfer to acquire, and his chief delight when he can manage it.
—Henry Brougham Farnie, 1857

[Allan Robertson's] entire nature was bent on being a golfer. It is yet told
on the links how Allan would rise betimes and, with shirt sleeves rolled up
for better muscular play, start alone for practice across the deserted links, still
wet with early dew. Allan has improved in his day on the old theories of golf and
to him are owing many of the improved methods and styles of the present game.
—*Dundee Advertiser*, 1859

**Its fascinations have always been gratefully
acknowledged, and not a few of its
worthier practitioners have from time to time
in prose and verse, rehearsed its praises.**
—Robert Clark, 1875

We do not presume to dictate but must observe
that the postures and gestures requisite for a full swing
are not particularly graceful when the player is clad in female dress.
—Lord Wellwood, 1890

It's an awful empty life hitting golf balls every day; you are not giving much service.
—Willie Auchterlonie, British Open Champion at 21 in 1893,
who then quit tournament golf and went into business as a clubmaker

Remember that it is always possible to "overgolf" yourself. Two rounds a day
is enough for any man with a week or more of solid golf in front of him.
—Horace G. Hutchinson, 1896

As a race [English women] are stronger and more athletic than we are,
and more accustomed to outdoor sports of all kinds. They have
a greater natural love for such things and probably will always excel in them;
so that while in time we may be able to furnish a few players who will
rank with England's best, still I doubt if the day will ever come
when we shall feel able to challenge "all England" with an "all American" team.
—Ruth Underhill, 1899

Golf, I have been told, is physically a better game for our sex than any other,
as it exercises a greater number of muscles without fear of over-exertion or strain.
—Issette Pearson, 1899

A SURPRISE
CHAMPION

Peggy Abbot, a member of the Chicago Golf Club, was visiting Paris in 1900 with her mother, who was also a keen golfer. Responding to an advertisement, they entered a nine-hole tournament in Compiegne, a Paris suburb that later became famous as the surrender site in both World War I and World War II. Shooting 47, Peggy won what she thought was the Paris city championship, while her mother came in seventh. Neither knew that Peggy had won an Olympic medal—the first given for women's golf. Peggy Abbot later married Finley Peter Dunne, the American satirist and creator of Mr. Dooley.

I drove a ball into the air.
It fell to earth I know not where.
But if I'd found it, I'll bet you,
I would have done that hole in two!

—Miles Bantock, 1901

Never since the days of Caesar has the British nation been subjected to such humiliation.

—Lord Northbourne, when Walter Travis was the first American
to win the British Amateur championship, 1904

Here's to the man with club in hand
Here's to the king of bogey land;
Here's to the clubs with outlandish names
And here's to GOLF the game of games!
—*The Father Gander Golf Book* (1909)

In the midst of that wilderness I chanced upon a somewhat chubby gentleman engaged in the pursuit of a small white ball, which, when he came within striking distance, he beat savagely with weapons of wood and iron.

That, sir, was my first sight of you, and my earliest acquaintance with the game of golf. I remember scanning the horizon for your keeper.
—Charles E. Van Loan, 1918

That youthful Cossack of the golf course, Light Horse
Harry Cooper . . . who plays this game of golf like a wild-eyed
cavalryman riding to a charge—a slashing, dashing,
hip-hooray young blade . . . came tearing up the last slope
of The Los Angeles Country Club toward sundown this afternoon,
his head bare, his carefully slicked back hair glinting with oil
and perspiration, and behind him panted several thousand men and
women as he trotted to his final shot, swinging his golf club like a sabre.
—Damon Runyan, on Harry Cooper's victory at the 1926 L.A. Open

CHAPTER THREE

FORE!
SHOTS FROM THE TEE

The right way to play golf is to go up and hit the bloody thing.
—George Duncan

Every golfer has an opinion, and players often can reduce their philosophies of the game to a quip. Besides, it's a whole lot easier to come up with a one-liner about the futility of golf than to perfect a one-piece swing. Golfing comedians such as Bob Hope may do a whole standup routine based on their last match, while the golf games of others—Gerald Ford's comes to mind—are a well-known joke in themselves.

Humor is as essential to the exigencies of golf as exaggeration and hopefulness are to the concepts of "the next big one" or "the one that got away" in fishing. Each voice in this chapter is as individual as each golfer's swing, and the shots land all over the fairway—and sometimes out of bounds.

The golf swing itself is perhaps the chief source of both frustration and humor in the game. The swing just may be humankind's most analyzed, photographed, written-, and talked-about physical movement, varying from the prodigious "Grip It and Rip It" method of John Daly, to the sweet, fluid sweeping motion of Fred Couples. Yet no swing is the right one for everyone, and one person's smooth follow-through could be another person's debilitating back injury. No kidding.

The two easiest shots in golf are the fourth putt
and the explosion shot off the tee.
—Ring Lardner

Golf swings are like snowflakes: there are no two exactly alike.
—Peter Jacobsen

The golf swing is like a suitcase into which
we are trying to pack one too many items.
—John Updike

He swings the club in a figure eight. If you didn't know better, you'd swear he was trying to kill snakes.
—Dave Hill

You can buy a country but you can't buy a golf swing.
It's not on the shelf.
—Gene Sarazen

Golf is a game of motion and rhythm, not of position and mechanics.
—Martin Hall

Good-looking form is one of the secrets of good golf. Look beautiful
and you'll play beautiful. However, some old codgers with whom
I play, play mighty ugly and beat the pants off me.
—Don Herold

It doesn't matter if you look like a beast before or after the hit,
as long as you look like a beauty at the moment of impact.
—Severiano Ballesteros

The best stroked putt in a lifetime does not bring the esthetic satisfaction
of a perfectly hit wood or iron shot. There is nothing to match the whoosh
and soar, the almost magical flight of a beautifully hit drive or 5-iron.
—Al Barkow

Golf is like art: it's impossible to be perfect.
—Sandra Palmer

It takes so long to accept that you can't always replicate your swing.
The only thing you can control is your attitude toward the next shot.
—Mark McCumber

Let the ball get in the way of the swing, instead of making the ball the object.
—Jack Burke, Sr.

A hit must be perfectly timed, but a swing will time itself.
—Grantland Rice

Swing easy, hit hard.
—Julius Boros

The only thing you should force in a golf swing is the club back into the bag.
—Byron Nelson

A golf ball is like a clock. Always hit it at six o'clock and make it go toward twelve o'clock. Just be sure you're in the same time zone.
—Chi Chi Rodriguez

I can airmail the golf ball, but sometimes I don't put the right address on it.
—Jim Dent (a famously long driver)

I only hit the ball about 220 [yards] off the tee, but I can always find it.
—Bonnie Lauer

LEE TREVINO,
"THE KING OF COURSE QUIPS"

In his day, the Texan golfer Lee Trevino, "Super Mex," was as celebrated as Tiger Woods for expanding the professional game to include members of minorities as he tore through his opponents, winning all the majors but the Masters. But he is nearly as famous for his charisma and sense of humor. His one-liners have ranged from swing advice ("There's only two things in the world you gotta do with your head down—golf and praying" and "You can talk to a fade, but a hook won't listen"), to advice on proper use of the one-iron ("When I'm on a course and it starts to rain and lightning, I hold up a one-iron, 'cause I know that even God can't hit a one-iron").

Today he has brought his powerful game and rapier wit to the Senior Tour, which he enthusiastically joined the minute he turned fifty, reasoning, "Why play with the flat bellies when you can play with the round bellies?" Some of his fellow pros, however, are jealous of the attention he gets for his charismatic reputation; Orville Moody has complained that "More people show up to watch Lee Trevino change shoes than watch me tee off."

I'm hitting the woods just great, but I'm having
a terrible time getting out of them.
—Harry Toscano

Playing golf is a little like carving a turkey:
it helps if you have your slice under control.
—Bob Orben

Hook: the addiction of fifty percent of all golfers.
Slice: the weakness of the other half.
—Jim Bishop

Practice Tee: the place where golfers go to convert
a nasty hook into a wicked slice.
—Henry Beard and Roy McKie

I don't say my golf is bad, but if I grew tomatoes, they'd come up sliced.
—Miller Barber

First you teach a golfer to hook the ball by using
his hands and arms properly. Then you teach him how to take
the hook away by using his body and legs properly.
—Harvey Penick

Once your mind knows you've mis-aimed,
your body gives up on making a good swing.
—Frank Beard

If you're stupid enough to whiff, you should be smart enough to forget it.
—Arnold Palmer

If you drink, don't drive. Don't even putt.
—Dean Martin

Nobody ever looked up and saw a good shot.
—Don Herold

I never did see the sense in keeping my head down.
The only reason I play golf at all is to see where the ball goes.
—Charles Price

The reason the pro tells you to keep your head down is so you can't see him laughing.
—Phyllis Diller

Wind, hole design and a hundred other factors in golf mean
that you never hit the same shot two times in a row.
—Phil Mickelson

In making a hole in one I stand with the feet fairly wide apart
and the weight evenly distributed on both heels. I use the interlocking grip,
a three-quarters swing, a thirty-five cent ball, and the regulation prayer.
I generally wear light underwear, as there is nothing that will upset a stroke
more than the itch that comes from a woolen or hair-lined undershirt at the
moment of the upswing, and prefer socks that are smart without being vulgar.
—H. I. Phillips

Man blames fate for other accidents
but feels personally responsible for a hole in one.
—Martha Beckman

In Japan, player who scores hole-in-one while
leading tournament always lose; it's proven jinx.
—Ayako Okamoto

When money's on the line, golf becomes like poker: you can play to win or you
can play not to lose. Or, if you don't have any real idea what the difference is,
you can do what most golfers and poker players do: play to lose.
They don't know that's what they're doing but the loss is just as inevitable
as if they had drawn four cards to a deuce kicker or used a putter off the tee.
—Turk Pipkin

Never bet [against] anyone you meet on the first tee who
has a deep suntan, a one-iron in his bag, and squinty eyes.
—Dave Marr

CHAPTER FOUR

THE ARCHITECTS

Golf architects can't play golf themselves
and make damn sure that no one else can.

— 20th-century American saying

To design and construct a golf course that is a joy to play for the most irredeemable hacker, yet a true test for the most gifted professional, is a feat at which only a select few succeed. But in the beginning, there were no golf course architects—or perhaps more accurately, God was the only architect. Along the eastern coast of Scotland, hardscrabble seacoast wastelands that were fit for nothing else became the first "links" (the Old English word *hlinc* means a ridge of land along the sea). Casual players and, later, club members merely inserted tees and holes into the existing terrain. Allan Robertson, a ball maker from the feathery period and the first true golf professional, also became the first golf architect when he remodeled the Old Course at St. Andrews in 1842. Six years later, the gutta-percha ball's longer drives and increased accuracy ushered in the era of classic course design, with longer, more challenging holes and a new generation of golf professionals-turned-architects to build them.

In 1893, Charles Blair Macdonald became the first American golf course architect when he designed the Chicago Golf Club, the first eighteen-hole course in the U.S. (He was the first U.S. Amateur Champion two years later.) Henry C. Fownes's design for Oakmont Country Club near Pittsburgh, completed in 1903, began the "penal style" of architecture—guided by its founder's principle that "a poorly played shot should result in a shot irrevocably lost." Fownes filled 350 traps on the course, nearly twenty per hole, with four inches of brown river-bottom sand. The evolved penal style, exemplified by the long career of Robert Trent Jones, also features multiple "dogleg" holes, water hazards, and out-of-bounds penalties.

The British influence on American golf course architecture continued well into the 1930s. Alister Mackenzie, a Scottish ex-physician, collaborated with Bobby Jones in the creation of the Augusta National Golf Club, home of the Masters and the prototype of the "strategic style" golf course. Golf became a thinker's game as well as one of technical skill because these courses offered more than one way to play each hole. The strategic is still the dominant course style, giving duffers a fighting chance while challenging champions.

The profession became formalized only in 1947, with the founding of the American Society of Golf Course Architects at Pinehurst, North Carolina. Since then, many champion players, notably Arnold Palmer and Jack Nicklaus, have become golf course designers, chiefly for resorts and developments. The newer "scenic style" of highly landscaped but not especially well thought-out holes reflects the real trend of golf course architecture today: as an aid to selling houses. Recently, "links"-style holes along the water have become retro-chic, at least in marketing brochures.

"The man who hates golfers" is what they call me.
They couldn't be more wrong. I design holes that are fun to play.
—Robert Trent Jones

The creator of golf holes must not only possess imagination
but a keen appreciation of the offerings of nature, and the art
of landscaping must be allied closely with that of the architect.
—A.W. Tillinghast

The real trick of golf course architecture
is to lure the golfer into a false sense of security.
—Peter Dye

The trick for the developer, as devised through
his architect, is to build something that is photogenically stunning,
however impractical, extravagant or absurd.
Never mind the golfer, that most gullible of all citizens.
—Peter Thomson

[Golf architects] don't build courses for people.
They build monuments to themselves.
—George Archer

We are business men and do not lay out courses for the benefit of our health, and if in fact we only consulted the interests of [scratch golfers] one percent of those who play golf we should soon cease to have a business, for no one would employ or recommend us. On the contrary we lay out courses for the enjoyment of all and sundry. If any one class receives more consideration than another it is the twelve handicap man, who is perhaps the mainstay of most clubs.

—W. Herbert Fowler

Every golfer worthy of the name should have some acquaintance with the principles of golf course design, not only for the betterment of the game, but for his own selfish enjoyment. Let him know a good hole from a bad one and the reasons for a bunker here and another there, and he will be a long way towards pulling his score down to respectable limits. When he has taught himself to study a hole from the point of view of the man who laid it out, he will be much more likely to play it correctly.

—Bobby Jones

Like pool, golf is primarily a game of position. The professional pool player never takes one shot at a time. He organizes a series of shots in his mind in order to sink all the balls on the table. The key is to get a good "leave" or an ideal position for the next shot.

—Robert Trent Jones, Jr.

The strategy of the golf course is the soul of the game. The spirit of golf is to dare a hazard, and by negotiating it reap a reward.

—George C. Thomas, Jr.

Undulation is the soul of golf.
—H. N. Wethered

Golf is a better game played downhill.
—Jack Nicklaus

His courses are like Jack [Nicklaus] himself:
grim and humorless, with sharp edges.
—Peter Thomson

[The Nicklaus-designed course in Grand Cypress, Florida] is like
one of those hot-air hand dryers in toilets. It's a great idea
and everybody uses it once, but never again. It takes too long.
—David Feherty

It is easier to replace the turf than to returf the place.
—Sign posted on a British golf course

He who insists on preserving a tree
where it spoils a shot should have nothing to say
about golf course construction.
—George C. Thomas, Jr.

**There is no such thing as a misplaced bunker.
Regardless of where a bunker may be,
it is the business of the player to avoid it.**
—Donald Ross

If I had my way, I'd never let the sand be raked. Instead,
I'd run a herd of elephants through the bunkers every morning.
—Charles Blair Macdonald

[Macdonald] was so rugged in his thinking that he probably
wore his tweed knickerbockers without any underwear.
—Charles Price

The sand putting green has gone where the woodbine twineth
and the dickey-bird pines for his mate. It has been
relegated to the limbo of forgotten things, along with Von Kluck,
rye highballs, and Willyum Jennings Bryan.
—Charles E. Van Loan

It should be remembered that golf started by the sea; it was played
on a type of country called 'links,' which is the link between
the sea and the land, and today most of our great golf courses are links,
but you cannot have links anywhere else but by the seaside.
—Lord Brabazon

Greens near the ocean break imperceptibly toward the sea.
—Ben Hogan

Where I play,
the greens always break toward the bar.
—George Gobel

The ideal golf course is one that will test all golfers equally
according to their respective abilities,
and at the same time give them an equal amount of pleasure.
—W. Herbert Fowler

The best way to build a golf course
is to start two hundred years ago.
—Peter Dobereiner

The best architects feel it to be their duty to make the path
to the hole as free as possible from annoying difficulties for the less
skillful golfers, while at the same time presenting to the
scratch players a route calling for the best shots at their command.
—Robert Hunter

THE PHILADELPHIA SCHOOL

In the years before World War I, Pennsylvania and southern New Jersey comprised the center of American golf course design and construction. The famous architects of the "Philadelphia School" included Henry C. Fownes, Hugh Wilson (who designed the Merion Golf Club in the suburbs of Philadelphia in 1912), A.W. Tillinghast (designer of Baltusrol in Springfield, New Jersey; Winged Foot in Mamaroneck, New York; and the San Francisco Golf Club), George Crump, and George C. Thomas, Jr. They all competed with and learned from one another, and shared in Tillinghast's credo that "It costs no more to follow nature than to ignore her; if you must introduce artificial elements into a golf course, make them appear natural."

Crump, a hotel owner in Philadelphia, founded Pine Valley Country Club in Clementon, New Jersey, in 1913, where he designed and built the ultimate penal course (with help from English architect Harry S. Colt), using $250,000 of his own money. When Crump died in 1918, Wilson finished the course. On Pine Valley's opening the next year, Charles Blair Macdonald pronounced it the finest golf course in the United States, a judgment still generally held. Thomas, who had designed the Spring Lake, New Jersey, course in 1910, moved to Southern California, where he finished The Los Angeles Country Club's North Course, designed by England's W. Herbert Fowler, and designed the Riviera Country Club and Bel-Air Country Club courses on his own. In 1927, Thomas also wrote the classic work *Golf Architecture in America: Its Strategy and Construction*.

The Seven Deadly Sins of Architecture: greens that don't drain;
greens that drain too much; greens too large for small shots;
greens too small for large shots; greens too freakish for any shot;
holes playing directly into the slopes of hills;
holes requiring climbs to higher levels too suddenly.
—A. W. Tillinghast

A good golf course is like good music. It does not necessarily appeal the first time one plays it.
—Alister Mackenzie

There are many bad long courses and many very good short courses,
and length has very little to do with merit.
—Harry S. Colt

Golf is not a fair game, so why build a fair course?
—Peter Dye

A great golf hole is one which puts a question mark
into a player's mind when he arrives on the tee to play it.
—Mackenzie Ross

Great golf courses should have at least one silly hole.
—Frank Hannigan

Every hole should be a demanding par and a comfortable bogey.
—Robert Trent Jones

[Robert] Trent Jones must have a permanent crick in his neck.
Every time he walks down a fairway, he's looking behind
him to see how he can make the hole longer.
—Gene Sarazen

All truly great golf courses have an almost supernatural finishing hole,
by way of separating the chokers from the strokers.
—Charles Price

The job of a finishing hole is as clearly defined as that
of a dance hall bouncer: It has to maintain order,
clear out the amateurs, preserve the dignity of the game.
—Jim Murray

**The first eighteen holes give a golf club
its reason to exist; the 19th gives it the money.**
—Robinson Murray

CHAPTER FIVE

HAMARATIA: THE BODY, MIND, AND SOUL OF THE GOLFER

Golf is a game to teach you about the messages from within,

about the subtle voices of the body-mind. And once you understand them you

can more clearly see your "hamaratia," the ways in which your approach

to the game reflects your entire life. Nowhere does a man go so naked.

—Michael Murphy

Golf is like a religion for some, and, like spiritual faith, not easily explained. That doesn't stop true zealots from trying to preach to and convert the pagan hordes. For the obsessed, the lure of golf borders on a gnostic mysticism: it contains the key of life, an inner truth incomprehensible even to the true believer's golf-widower or -widow, not to mention the outside world.

The mystical golfer often affects, or actually reflects, an inner calm like that found in devotees of certain martial arts and embodies a puzzling lack of competitive spirit. The game reached its apotheosis as a New Age phenomenon with Michael Murphy's 1970 book, *Golf in the Kingdom*, a kind of bible for many male baby-boomers. For the truly committed—or perhaps those who *should* be committed—expensive weekend seminars are available to study this philosophy.

To others, golf is a "bug" or a virus, something that has infected their physical being and therefore also cannot be explained away. But at least this "physical" affliction can be described, sort of. Physical rationales tend to be feeble: golf is good outdoor exercise (except for those who ride in carts); it's an escape to the country from the pressures of work (except for those who take along their cellular telephones); or it's a social game in pleasant surroundings (at least in and around the 19th hole). Whoever the golfer, there *is* something special about striding out on the tee and striking for the pin . . . to find either the Nirvana of the green or the Hades of the sandtrap.

The pleasure derived from hitting the ball dead center
on the club is comparable only to one or two
other pleasures that come to mind at the moment.
—Dinah Shore

What other people may find in poetry
or art museums, I find in the flight of a good drive.
—Arnold Palmer

The beauty about golf is the ball doesn't know how big you are.
—Claude Harmon

Your final goal is to convert your athletic swing to pure instinct
rather than conscious thought.
—David Leadbetter

They were real golfers, for real golf is a thing of the spirit,
not of mere mechanical excellence of stroke.
—P. G. Wodehouse

Golf is a spiritual game. It's like Zen.
You have to let your mind take over.
—Amy Alcott

**A great round of golf is like a terrible round.
You drift into a zone, and it is hard to break out of it.**
—Al Geiberger

The zone is the ability to give 110 percent of your attention and your focus
to the shot. When I'm on the tee, I'll see a divot in the fairway
and try to run my ball over that divot—and succeed. That's the zone.
—Nick Price

**When I'm in this state, everything is pure,
vividly clear. I'm in a cocoon of concentration.**
—Tony Jacklin

When I play my best golf, I feel as if I'm in a fog . . . standing back
watching the earth in orbit with a golf club in my hands.
—Mickey Wright

I've learned to trust the subconscious. My instincts have never lied to me.
—Tiger Woods

When I'm in a zone, I don't think about he shot or the wind
or the distance or the gallery or anything; I just pull a club and swing.
—Mark Calcavecchia

As far as swing and techniques are concerned, I don't know diddly-squat.
When I'm playing well, I don't even take aim.
—Fred Couples

**You play your best golf by just reacting
to the target. If you are focused on the target,
you aren't thinking about anything bad happening.**
—Davis Love III

In addition to the unconscious vigor of body and mind imparted by golf,
the social amenities arising therefrom are of unquestionable
therapeutic value, since the genial influences of the game by expanding
the ideas tend to promote the good fellowship that comes
from diversion and sensuous amusement, and by oiling the wheels of life,
so to speak, makes them go on with rattling glee.
—Dr. Irving C. Rosse

Although golf is a game played with other people,
it is essentially an individualistic, and therefore a lonely, experience.
The presence and demeanor of the other people involved
generally inject a spirit of camaraderie into the game. But, at root,
the overt show of fellowship is a disguise masking an inherent
a loneliness of endeavor often so intense as to be almost existential.
—Dr. David Morely

On the golf course you can't feel sorry for anybody.
You have to try to win the golf tournament.
You're not beating the guy you're playing against,
you're beating the course. And that's probably life.
I've got to live with it, and they've got to live with it.
—Ernie Els

**In a gin'ral way, all I can say about it is
it's a kind iv game iv ball that ye play with ye'eer
own worst inimy, which is ye'ersilf.**
—Finley Peter Dunne

I know of no better cure for illusions
of grandeur than a game of golf.
—Dr. W. Beran Wolfe

The poetic temperament is the worst for golf.
It dreams of brilliant drives, iron shots laid dead, and long putts holed,
while in real golf success waits for him who takes care
of the foozles and leaves the fine shots to take care of themselves.
—Sir Walter Simpson

It is a game in which the whole temperamental strength
of one side is hurled against the strength of the other, and the two human
natures are pressing bitterly and relentlessly against each other
from the first moment of the game to the last. It is the whole man,
mind and body. That is the meaning of the temperamental
factor in golf, and that is why a great match at golf is great indeed.
—Henry Leach

Your ego is everything.
And if you don't get that pumped up regularly you can't last.
—Dave Marr

Golf is the ego and id in a playoff that never ends.
—David Noonan

THE GENTLEMAN'S SPIRIT

P.G. Wodehouse, an English-born but American-based writer best known for his Jeeves and Bertie Wooster stories and his musical comedies with Guy Bolton, was a keen golfer who often wrote in novels and short stories about the game. Wodehouse's work always reflected his own passionate love-hate relationship with the game.

In *The Clicking of Cuthbert*, he wrote: "What earthly good is golf? Life is stern and life is earnest. We live in a practical age. All around us we see foreign competition making itself unpleasant. And we spend our time playing golf! What do we get out of it? Is golf of any use? That's what I'm asking you. Can you name me a single case where devotion to this pestilential pastime has done a man any practical good?"

Staying in the present is the key to any golfer's game:
once you start thinking about a shot you just messed up or what you have
to do on the next nine to catch somebody, you're lost.

—Paul Azinger

If just some of the principles that keep players out of trouble
in their day-to-day affairs were applied to their golf game,
their handicaps would drop drastically.

—Greg Norman

I'm about five inches from being an outstanding golfer.
That's the distance my left ear is from my right.

—Ben Crenshaw

You have to train the mind for success.
When I first joined the tour,
I didn't think I was as good as I was.
Now my mental has caught up with my physical.

—Calvin Peete

At golf you've got to be mentally alert.
You can't lean against a tree that isn't there.

—Doug Sanders

Action before thought is the ruination of most of your shots.
—Tommy Armour

Serenity is knowing that your worst shot is going to be pretty good.
—Johnny Miller

Confidence is everything.
From there, it's a small step to winning.
—Craig Stadler

Prepare for success, accept what happens,
then get ready for your next shot.
—Davis Love, Jr.

Every great golfer has learned to think positively,
to assume the success and not the failure of a shot,
to disregard misfortune and to accept disaster,
and never to indulge the futility of remorse and blame.
These are the hardest lessons of all.
—Pat Ward-Thomas

A bad attitude is worse than a bad swing.
—Payne Stewart

If you want to beat somebody on the golf course, just get him mad.
—Dave Williams

Golf cannot be played in anger, or in any mood of emotional excess.
Half the golf balls struck by amateurs are hit if not in rage
surely in bewilderment, or gloom, or in cynicism, or even hysterically—
all of those emotional excesses must be contained by the professional.
Which is why, balance is one of the essential ingredients
of golf, professionals invariably trudge phlegmatically around the course—
whatever emotions are seething within—with the grim
yet placid and bored look of cowpokes, slack-bodied in their saddles,
who have been tending the same herd for two months.
—George Plimpton

The average golfer doesn't play golf; he attacks it.
—Jackie Burke

When you reflect on the combination of characteristics that golf demands
of those who would presume to play it, it is not surprising that golf has never
had a truly great player who was not also a person of extraordinary character.
—Frank D. (Sandy) Tatum, Jr.

I try to be semi-humble. If I started going around
saying how good I was, everything would go wrong.
—Johnny Miller

CHAPTER SIX

RULES, ETIQUETTE, AND OTHER LOST ARTS

Golf is a game in which you yell "fore," shoot six and write down five.

—Paul Harvey

Few texts this side of the Bible are as widely-cited and seldom-read as the rules of golf. Even so, it was only after centuries of casual play that the Honourable Company of Edinburgh Golfers set down the first rules of the game in 1744. There were thirteen in number, and no penalties were provided if the rules were broken. Ten years later, the Royal and Ancient Golf Club of St. Andrews was chartered by George II on links that had been in use since at least 1552. From that day to this, the "R & A" has been considered the "cradle" of the game of golf, and it immediately took over stewardship of the rules in 1754. Twelve of the original thirteen rules have survived virtually intact.

In 1897 the R & A formed The Rules of Golf Committee. The United States Golf Association had been formed three years earlier, and while it generally followed its Scottish role model where rules were concerned, there were noticeable divergences. In 1921, the Royal and Ancient and the U.S.G.A. jointly revised *The Rules of Golf.* The golf ball, which had been slightly different in the two countries, was limited in diameter to 1.62 inches, and in weight to 1.62 ounces. Lost balls, unplayable balls, and balls out of bounds now produced uniform penalties of distance and stroke. Clubs were limited worldwide to fourteen, the standard set being four woods, eight irons numbered two through nine, a wedge, and a putter.

Delegates from the R & A and the U.S.G.A. meet twice a year to discuss and adopt proposed changes in the rules. The rule book is republished quadrennially, and begins with a section on etiquette. Almost ten pages are devoted to distinguishing between amateur and professional status, and another five pages delineate the design of clubs. Recently, a delegate from the Phillipines at the R & A/U.S.G.A rules conference wanted to know if cobras counted as "an outside agency" (covered by Rule 19) or a "loose impediment" (Rule 23).

Local variations in rules do occur. One Arizona course allows a free drop two club lengths away from a rattlesnake. A course in Africa permits a free drop from hippopotamus footprints, and requires golfers to yield to elephants. Another in Nairobi offers players relief from crocodiles, monkeys, zebras, and other wild animals that might be on the fairway. No course yet built offers players relief from the vagaries of poor play, vexation, and the occasional expletives that accompany the game, wherever its played.

Golf . . . is the only game in the world in which a precise knowledge
of the rules can earn one a reputation for bad sportsmanship.
—Patrick Campbell

Golf may be . . . a sophisticated game. At least, it is usually
played with the outward appearance of great dignity.
It is, nevertheless, a game of considerable passion, either of the explosive
type, or that which burns inwardly and sears the soul.
—Bobby Jones

Golf was invented by some Scotsman who hit a ball, with a stick,
into a hole in the ground. The game today is exactly the same,
except that it now takes some ninety-odd pages of small type to ensure
that the ball is hit with the stick into the hole in the ground without cheating.
—A. S. Graham

Golf is the hardest game in the world to play and the easiest to cheat at.
—Dave Hill

If there is any larceny in a man, golf will bring it out.
—Paul Gallico

The only way of really finding out a man's true character is to play golf with
him. In no other walk of life does the cloven hoof so quickly display itself.
—P. G. Wodehouse

[Golf] taught me perseverance, it taught me not to cheat—no easy thing
for a boy when he's two down and his ball is deep in the woods.

—James "Scotty" Reston

Golf is based on honesty. Where else would
someone admit to a seven on an easy par three?

—Jimmy Demaret

Golf appeals to the idiot in us and the child. What child does not grasp
the simple pleasure-principle of miniature golf? Just how childlike golf
players become is proven by their frequent inability to count past five.

—John Updike

I've seen lifelong friends drift apart over golf just because
one could play better, but the other counted better.

—Stephen Butler Leacock

The income tax has made liars out of more Americans than golf.

—Will Rogers

**It's good sportsmanship not to pick up
lost balls while they are still rolling.**

—Mark Twain

If you think it's hard meeting new people,
try picking up the wrong golf ball.
—Jack Lemmon

**You might as well praise a man for not robbing a
bank as to praise him for playing [golf] by the rules.**
—Bobby Jones

It has been estimated that a golfer's chances of making a hole in one are
much greater than the probability that he will read the rules of the game.
—Herb Graffis

If a man is notified he has been appointed to serve on the rules committee
for a certain tournament he should instantly remember
that he must attend an important business meeting in Khartoum.
—Herbert Warren Wind

**If you call on God to improve the results
of a shot while it is still in motion, you are using
"an outside agency" and are subject
to appropriate penalties under the rules of golf.**
—Henry Longhurst

THE THWACKER'S TALE

In the summer of 1899, Edward B. Tufts, the foremost sporting goods merchant in Los Angeles and a founder of The Los Angeles Country Club, was playing over a newly built golf course at Santa Monica-by-the-Sea. Tufts sliced badly to the right on his drive from the third tee. His ball stopped in front of a grazing milk cow in an adjacent field. Tufts sidled up just in time to see her scoop his ball up into her mouth. After his opponent had teed off, Tufts untethered the cow and prodded her with his club all the way to the third green, where he thwacked her until she disgorged his ball near the hole. Neatly holing the putt, Tufts gleefully announced that he had made the hole in two strokes—while his opponent had taken seven—and claimed victory. The friend was not having any of it: "You made it in 39! You hit the cow 37 times, for I counted every stroke." Tufts conceded the hole, but press coverage of the incident reached as far away as Toledo and Chicago, and sealed his reputation as a colorful golfing figure.

In competition, during gunfire or while bombs are falling, players may
take cover without penalty for ceasing play. The positions
of known delayed-reaction bombs are marked by red flags at a reasonably,
but not guaranteed, safe distance therefrom. . . . A ball moved
by enemy action may be replaced, or if lost or "destroyed" a ball may
be dropped not nearer the hole without penalty. A player whose
stroke is affected by the simultaneous explosion of a bomb may play another
ball from the same place. Penalty, one stroke.
—Temporary World War II rule at the Richmond Golf Club, outside London

I love it here in the United States. In Japan, I have no privacy.
In the States, I can have a hole in my jeans and nobody will notice.
—Ayako Okamato

If [Southern folks] know you are working at home, they think nothing of walking right in for coffee. But they wouldn't dream of interrupting you at golf.
—Harper Lee

I know that in golf I'm a black face walking through
a white man's world. It can make you jittery.
But I've reached the point I don't feel like an outsider.
I know half the people I meet.
—Jim Thorpe

I never pray on a golf course. Actually, the Lord answers
my prayers everywhere except on the course.
—Rev. Billy Graham

Golf courses are the best places to observe ministers,
because none of them are above cheating a bit.
—John D. Rockefeller, Sr.

Good golfing temperament falls between taking it with a grin or shrug and throwing a fit.
—Sam Snead

Always throw clubs ahead of you.
That way you don't have to waste energy going back to pick them up.
—Tommy Bolt

I don't play well enough to be allowed to throw my clubs.
—Lou Holtz

Golfers don't fist fight. They cuss a lot. But they wouldn't punch anything
or anybody. They might hurt their hands and have to change their grip.
—Dan Jenkins

Out of the mouths of America's most clean-cut
group of athletes—except, perhaps, bowlers—comes a rich vein of slang
that makes the hyped-up wild men of the NFL seem bland.
—Thomas Boswell

If profanity had an influence on the flight of the ball, the game would be played far better than it is.
—Horace G. Hutchinson

I've had words come into my mind while I was digging
in a bunker that I never realized I knew. . . .
I have never felt better than when I gave up the game.
—Nunnally Johnson

But since I cannot play at golf
Unless I swear a wee,
I'll give it up. "What, golf?" they cried.
Nae, mon—the ministry.
—19th-century Scottish rhyme

The only time I talk on a golf course is to my caddie—and only
then to complain when he gives me the wrong club.
—Seve Ballesteros

Perhaps the best way of curing yourself of the tendency to become
irritable and morose when you are playing badly is to pull yourself up
and think how objectionable and ridiculous other people look
when they are in the same state.
—H. J. Whigham

Moderation is essential in all things, madam,
but never in my life have I failed to beat a teetotaler.
—Harry Vardon

When you are ahead, don't take it easy, kill them.
After the finish, then be a sportsman.
—Earl Woods, giving advice to his son, Tiger

I play with friends, but we don't play friendly games.
—Ben Hogan

Stroke play is a better test of golf,
but match play is a better test of character.
—Joe Carr

If your adversary is a hole or two down,
there is no serious cause for alarm in his complaining of a severely
sprained wrist. . . . Should he happen to win the next hole,
these symptoms will in all probability become less troublesome.
—Horace G. Hutchinson

Golf is not a game you can rush.
For every stroke you try to force out of her,
she is going to extract two strokes in return.
—Dave Hill

If the average American player would only realize how much
easier it is to play well when he is swinging along at a good rate,
he would surely gird up his loins and walk a little faster.
—H. J. Whigham

It is a law of nature that everybody plays a hole badly when playing through.
—Bernard Darwin, grandson of Charles

Nothing goes down slower than a golf handicap.
—Bobby Nichols

Golf isn't like other sports where you can take a player out if he's having a bad day. You have to play the whole game.
—Phil Blackmar

If you play a bad hand of bridge, people will snap at you
and call you names and never invite you to their homes again.
But if you dub around at golf, you only arouse a storm of friendly laughter.
—Dr. W. Beran Wolfe

CHAPTER SEVEN

ADVICE FROM
THE GURUS

There are three ways of learning golf: by study, which is the most wearisome;
by imitation, which is the most fallacious; and by experience, which is the most bitter.

—Robert H. K. Browning

Since 95 percent of all golfers never break 100, and even the finest pros have their really bad days, advice—from caddies, opponents, partners, mothers, and, yes, even "Dear Abby"—has always been part of the game. The main reason for this is that nothing about the game of golf is innate to anyone. Even natural athletes have to acquire those contortions. So nobody is a born expert. And everybody these days seems to claim he is.

Golfing advice too often comes from the "those-who-can't-do" school of teaching—and most of them are strangers. Hit your ball into the rough, or miss a putt after seven straight holes of beating the pants off the rest of the pickup foursome a strange country club found for you, and these duffers will volunteer to tell you all that's wrong with your game.

Even the most successful pros don't always make the best surrogate teachers, however, on videotape or otherwise, with Palmer, Nicklaus, and Norman the exceptions. Similarly, most club pros may be great teachers, but are rarely the best golfers, even on their home courses. And most of them don't go out on a pro circuit. The Scottish-born Tommy Armour, who achieved all of his success in America, was one of the relatively few successful touring professionals who became a topflight teacher. "The Silver Scot's" classic book, *How to Play Your Best Golf All the Time*, is still a standard.

Precisely because golf is an acquired skill rather than a natural one, it requires even more dedication and practice than most games to get it right. This is not the advice that most hackers want to hear. Although golf is a game of the heart and mind, mastering the basics—stance, grip, and swing—is essential. Stance may vary with size of the player, and the overlapping "Vardon Grip" isn't always the answer—Sarazen and Nicklaus did all right with an interlocking grip. And the best swing is simply the one that hits the ball straight and far. Even the pros need to seek corrections from their teachers.

**All golfers, men and women,
professional and amateur,
are united by one thing—
their desire to improve.**
—Judy Rankin

One thing that's always available on a golf course is advice.
If you play like I do, you think everybody knows something you don't
know. If I see a bird fly over, I think he's going to tell me something.
—Buddy Hackett

We've got a society now looking for answers anywhere.
They might go to a car wash to take a lesson.
—Jackie Burke

**Golf is not a particularly natural game.
Like sword-swallowing, it has to be learned.**
—Brian Swarbrick

Reverse every natural instinct you have and do just the opposite
of what you are inclined to do and you will probably come
very close to having a perfect golf swing.
—Ben Hogan

Ben Hogan just knows something about hitting the golf ball the rest of us don't know.

—Mike Souchak

Rhythm and timing we all must have,
yet no one knows how to teach either.

—Bobby Jones

If you expect a miracle, you should expect to pay for one.

—Derek Hardy, a teaching pro, on why he charged $140 for 13 lessons and $1000 for one

The professional, aside from being your teacher,
has your interests at heart. . . . He will listen to your lamentations—why
the putt didn't drop on the 18th, or why you hooked in the rough on the 11th.
He will be your father confessor of golf. Take your troubles to him.

—Sam Snead

No one becomes a champion without help.

—Johnny Miller

The biggest thing [sports psychologist Bob Rotella] did for me—the key
to my success—was to get me to try to hole every shot, to try
to focus wholly on knocking every shot into the cup from the fairway.

—Ian Baker-Finch

In Europe, we think it's funny that Tour players travel
with a sports psychologist or call one after every round.
—Ernie Els

I've never had a coach in my life;
when I can find one who can beat me, I'll listen.
—Lee Trevino

It is an unwise pro that beats his only pupil.
—Gerald Batchelor

Being left-handed is a big advantage.
No one knows enough about your swing
to mess you up with advice.
—Bob Charles

Golf is a difficult game, but it's a little easier if you trust your instincts.
It's too hard a game to try to play like somebody else.
—Nancy Lopez

If you can get the ball in the hole regularly by standing on your head,
then keep right on—and don't listen to advice from anyone.
—John Jacobs

Golf is the most over-taught and least-learned human endeavor. If they taught sex the way they teach golf, the human race would have died out years ago.
—Jim Murray

There has been criticism that some professional golfers do not know how to teach. In defense of my competent colleagues in professional golf, I must point out that many pupils don't know how to take a lesson.
—Tommy Armour

When they have an attention span that they can take instruction: I've always defined that as when they can play three holes without chasing a frog, and that's about an hour.
—Jack Nicklaus, asked when kids should start playing golf (he began at age ten)

Let's face it. [In learning about golf, your] child is learning about life. The by-products of golf are integrity, responsibility and patience.
—Earl Woods, father of Tiger Woods

[My father, Domingo] persuaded rather than pushed me at golf. He always told me not to be afraid if I was behind in a tournament, that I could go out and shoot another good round. If I blew a hole he would tell me to forget it and go on to the next one, I couldn't bring it back.
—Nancy Lopez

THE TEACHER'S TEACHER

Golf instruction books number in the hundreds—virtually all of them advocating the same overlapping grip and basic techniques—with the number of how-to-golf videos rapidly gaining all the time. But the late Harvey Penick, the legendary University of Texas coach, has long stood out among the crowd of golf gurus. His classic work, *Harvey Penick's Little Red Book* (compiled with Bud Shrake), is a compendium of his teachings, and is the best-selling sports instruction book of all time.

In his writings and teachings, Penick stressed the necessity not only of practice, but good practice: "In golf your strengths and weaknesses will always be there. If you could improve your weaknesses, you would improve your game. The irony is that most people prefer to practice their strengths." In order to improve these weaknesses, the golfer has "to make corrections in your game a little bit at a time. It's like taking your medicine: a few aspirin will probably cure what ails you, but the whole bottle could kill you."

Penick also stressed that the game should be approached athletically, with vigor: "Very early in our time together I try to get my pupils to hit the ball hard, even with the short irons. I believe if you start off in the game hitting the ball easy, you generally will keep it up. Your muscles learn the slow pace. You will always lack distance. Sometimes it takes longer to unlearn than it does to learn."

When you top a drive into a bunker or miss a short putt at a critical point
of the match, remember that you are playing a game for amusement,
even if you are desperately keen to win, which you have every right to be.
Tell yourself that your only chance of winning lies in forgetting past errors.
—H. J. Whigham

A long time ago I asked my teacher what the best exercise was for golf.
He said simply, "hitting golf balls."
—Larry Miller

Exercise will build up your body, but it won't do your score any good.
—Bobby Nichols

Golf should be played, not practiced.
—Billy Casper

Practicing is my meditation.
Some golfers like to fish and others read. I like to hit golf balls.
—Lee Trevino

The more I practice, the luckier I get.
—Gary Player

I take the revolutionary view that all this talk about the virtues of practice,
for the average club golfer at any rate, is a snare and a delusion.
"Practice makes perfect," they say. Of course, it doesn't. For the vast
majority of golfers it merely consolidates imperfection.
—Henry Longhurst

Your objective in golf is to groove your swing,
to make it so natural that you could hit a ball blindfolded.
—Johnny Farrell

Relax? How can anybody relax and play golf? You have to grip the club, don't you?
—Ben Hogan

Only one golfer in a thousand grips the club lightly enough.
—Johnny Miller

Stand firm and don't sway or look up.
—Harold Hilton

The golfer who stands at the ball as rigid as a statue
usually becomes a monumental failure.
—Dick Aultman

I never go past parallel; I think people look at me and say,
"That's the way I want to hit the ball."
—Tiger Woods

Be patient. Acquiring finesse takes time.
—Amy Alcott

Never give a golfer an ultimatum unless you're prepared to lose.
—"Dear Abby" (Abigail Van Buren), to a wife complaining of her husband's golf addiction

When your husband comes home with cockleburs in the cuffs of his pants, don't ask him what his score was.
—Sam Snead

If you need par, go for a birdie,
because if you don't get the birdie
you should hopefully get the par.
—Nick Faldo

Keep on hitting it straight until the wee ball goes in the hole.
—James Braid

Thinking must be the hardest thing we do in golf,
because we do so little of it.
—Harvey Penick

The trouble with me is I think too much.
I always said you have to be dumb to play good golf.
—JoAnne Carner

Give me a man with big hands and big feet and no brains,
and I'll make a golfer out of him.
—Walter Hagen

All good players have good hands,
and I'm afraid you have to be born with them.
—Dave Stockton

Bad golf is played with the shoulders and the body;
good golf is played with the hands.
—Gene Sarazen

You have the hands, now play with your heart.
—Roberto De Vicenzo, to Seve Ballesteros before he won the 1979 British Open

CHAPTER EIGHT

HAZARDS

Hazards are like spices that a designer sprinkles on a course to give it flavor.
—Robert Trent Jones, Jr.

The Bogey Man, or Colonel Bogey, was a golf course ghost who was blamed for messing up scores (especially putts for par) in England in the late 1800s. In the 1890s, Americans adopted "bogey" to mean one shot above the course standard score for a hole, leaving "par," which had been a nebulous English concept for several years, to mean the standard score, and their golfing heirs to curse the Colonel's ghost evermore. Though such specters are a rare impediment for today's golfer, most duffers are all too familiar with the haunting bogey, or the double-bogey, or worse. Still, bunkers and bodies of water are the most common deliberate impediments to a smooth round, though trees and rocks also are just naturally in the way.

A sand trap is called a bunker from the Scottish word *bonker*, a chest-like box in which coal was kept, usually dug into the side of a hill. Sheep or cattle grazing near the dunes on early links courses created a similar depression in the sand. While most sand traps, or bunkers, today are created, many in Scotland and elsewhere are still natural. A 100-yard expanse of scrub brush and sand on Number Seven at the legendary Pine Valley course in New Jersey's Pine Barrens is called "Hell's Half Acre," and is enshrined in *The Guinness Book of World Records* as the planet's biggest bunker.

Water hazards likewise were all natural in the beginning, from the traditional Highland lochs to the barrancas of Southern California. And some of them were intended to be incidental to the action. The 13th rule of the Honourable Company of Edinburgh Golfers in 1744 was a local one applying only to that course: "Neither Trench, Ditch or Dyke, made for the presentation of the Links, nor the Scholar's Holes or the Soldier's Lines, Shall be accounted a Hazard. But the ball is to be taken out and Tee'd and play'd with any Iron Club." Today, so-called "lateral hazards," man-made bodies of water that are parallel to the direction of play, provide great sport, at least for architects, and have recently made the water ball retriever one of the fastest-selling items of equipment. The current Rule 26 details the convoluted manner of playing out of a lateral hazard.

Though most course hazards are meant to be inert (although scenic designs often incorporate fountains and waterfalls), others such as crazed players and other wild animals are more difficult to negotiate. Tipsy golfcart drivers along the path and poison ivy, oak, or sumac in the rough may irritate a bit, while hornets' nests, swarms of mosquitoes, prowling coyotes, the odd ravenous wolf, and even the occasional alligator are sometimes also there for the stumbling upon. In addition, three thousand golfers each year get struck by lightning, most suffering only a mild shock while others are felled from the game for good. Though none of these dangers are technically "hazards" (even a falling tree limb is merely an "impediment"), they help to make the game of golf at times as much of a survivalist experience physically as it always is mentally.

For the golfer, Nature loses her significance. Larks, the casts of worms,
the buzzing of bees, and even children are hateful. . . . Rain
comes to be regarded solely in its relation to the putting greens; the daisy
is detested, botanical specimens are but "hazards," twigs "break clubs."
Winds cease to be east, south, west or north. They are ahead,
behind, sideways. And the sky is dark, according to the state of the game.
—Sir Walter Simpson

The object of a bunker or trap is not only to punish a physical mistake,
to punish lack of control, but also to punish pride and egotism.
—Charles Blair Macdonald

If your opponent is playing several shots in vain attempts to extricate
himself from a bunker, do not stand near him and audibly
count his strokes. It would be justifiable homicide if he wound up
his pitiable exhibition by applying his niblick to your head.
—Harry Vardon

My dear, did you ever stop to think what a lovely bunker you would make?
—Walter Hagen, to a famous opera diva

I stayed in the bunker until I made one.
They had to bring me cocktails and dinner.
—JoAnne Carner, on how she developed her sand game

Golf's three ugliest words: still your shot.
—Dave Marr

If your adversary is badly bunkered, there is no rule against your standing
over him and counting his strokes aloud, with increasing gusto
as their number mounts up; but it will be a wise precaution to arm yourself
with the niblick before doing so, so as to meet him on equal terms.
—Horace G. Hutchinson

**Mediocre players are just out there
messing up the sand traps.**
—Lloyd Mangrum

The good chip is like the good sand trap shot: it's your secret weapon.
It allows you to whistle while you walk in the dark alleys of golf.
—Tommy Bolt

The difference between a sand trap and water is the difference between a car
crash and an airplane crash. You have a chance of recovering from a car crash.
—Bobby Jones

I've lost balls in every hazard and on every course I've tried,
but when I lose a ball in the ball washer, it's time to take stock.
—Milton Gross

NON-TRADITIONAL HAZARDS

When faced with circumstances that the founding fathers of the rules of golf never saw on the links of Scotland, some of the golf world's more exotic courses have had to adapt the game. The exceptional hazards that the adventure golfers have faced have spurred the creativity of the Rules Committees of clubs the world over. Here are two of the most intriguing:

During the 1950s at the Nyanza Club, in British East Africa (now Kenya), a posted sign advised players that "If a ball comes to rest in dangerous proximity to a hippopotamus or crocodile, another ball may be dropped at a safe distance, no nearer the hole, without penalty."

The Royal Selanger Golf Club near Kuala Lumpur, Malaysia—which is built on an ancient Chinese burial ground—has this morbidly amusing local rule: "You cannot ground your club in addressing your ball, or move anything, no matter how loose or dead it may be."

If the water is rough in Santander Bay you fight harder in the boat.
You do not give up.
—Seve Ballesteros, son of a fisherman

Golf giveth and golf taketh away.
But it taketh away a hell of a lot more than it giveth.
—Simon Hobday

The golfer has more enemies than any other athlete. He has fourteen
clubs in his bag, all of them different; eighteen holes to play,
all of them different, every week; and all around him are sand, trees,
grass, water, wind, and 143 other players. In addition,
the game is fifty percent mental, so his biggest enemy is himself.
—Dan Jenkins

I think it's true that we create our own pressure.
If you think about water to the right and a trap to the left and all the things
that can go wrong, then you're creating your own pressure.
—Tom Weiskopf

Don't worry about par. The practice of printing
par figures is literally a mental hazard.
—Bobby Jones

Of all the hazards, fear is the worst.
—Sam Snead

The person I fear most in the last two rounds is myself.
—Tom Watson

You have to take this game through so many labyrinths of the mind,
past all the traps—like, will my masculinity be threatened
if I hit the ball well and still shoot 72?
—Mac O'Grady

Out on the golf course, factors such as wind speed,
pin position, distance to the flag, and any hazards
can play havoc with your decision making.
—Ernie Els

If you pick up a golfer and hold it close to your ear, like a conch shell, and listen, you will hear an alibi.
—Fred Beck

The toughest thing for most people to learn in golf
is to accept bad holes—and then forget about them.
—Gary Player

YOU SHOULD HAVE SEEN
THE BUNKERS ON THAT COURSE!

In 1971, American astronaut Alan Shepard brought along his six-iron and some golf balls in the Apollo capsule for his moon landing. As fellow astronaut Ed Mitchel watched, Shepard teed off on the lunar landscape.

As he struck the ball, Shepard narrated into his helmet, "There we go! Miles and miles and miles!"

Mitchel, who was unimpressed, quipped, "It looks like a slice to me, Al."

Shepard—like most duffers—was quick to create an alibi. On his return to Earth, he explained: "Because of the cumbersome suit I was wearing, I couldn't make a very good pivot on the swing, and I had to hit the ball with just one hand. It would normally have gone about 30 yards. Up there it went 200. My second shot was a shank. It went 40 or 50 yards. A ball won't hook or slice on the moon because it has no atmosphere, so this was a pure shank."

Like most professional golfers, I have a tendency to remember
my poor shots a shade more vividly than the good ones.
—Ben Hogan

If you hit a bad shot, just tell yourself it is great to be alive, relaxing and
walking around on a beautiful golf course. The next shot will be better.
—Al Geiberger

One bad shot does not make a losing score.
—Gay Brewer

I expect to make at least seven mistakes a round.
Therefore, when I make a bad shot, I don't worry about it.
It's just one of those seven.
—Walter Hagen

You tend to get impatient with poor shots or less-than-perfect shots,
but you have to remember less-than-perfect shots win Opens.
They are part of the game, and you have to learn to deal with them.
—Curtis Strange

I've quit worrying about poor shots. I just tell myself,
"Relax, Bozo. If you can't have fun, you shouldn't be out here."
—Patty Sheehan

**You can talk about strategy all you want,
but what really matters is resiliency.**

—Hale Irwin

Golf is a game that is measured in yards, but the difference
between a hit and a miss is calipered in micro-millimeters.

—"Champagne" Tony Lema

When I first came out on tour, I swung all out on every tee shot.
My drives finished so far off line, my pants were grass-stained at the knees.

—Fuzzy Zoeller

The longer the grass, the shorter the temper.

—Gerald Batchelor

It could be worse; I could be allergic to beer.

—Greg Norman, on discovering his allergy to grass

**Ben Crenshaw hits in the woods so often
he should get an orange hunting jacket.**

—Tom Weiskopf

Once when I was golfing in Georgia I hooked the ball into a swamp.
I went in after it and found an alligator wearing a shirt
with a picture of a little golfer on it.
—Buddy Hackett

Playing with your spouse on the golf course runs almost as great a marital
risk as getting caught playing with someone else's anywhere else.
—Peter Andrews

If I didn't have to worry about these things [bras and girdles], I could really hit it a mile.
—Babe Didrikson Zaharias

I'll take a two-shot penalty,
but I'll be damned if I'm going to play the ball where it lies.
—Elaine Johnson, when her ball bounced from a tree into her bra

The game was easy for me as a kid, and I had to play a while to find out how hard it is.
—Raymond Floyd

Growing old is mandatory.
Growing up is optional.
—Tom Wargo

Every round I play,
I shorten my life by two years.
—Tommy Nakajima

When you get up there in years,
the fairways get longer and the holes get smaller.
—Bobby Locke

There's just no way to make the hole look bigger.
—Tommy Armour

These are the hazards of golf: the unpredictability of your own body
chemistry, the rub of the green on the courses, the wind and the weather,
the bee that lands on your ball or on the back of your neck while you
are putting, the sudden noise while you are swinging, the whole problem
of playing the game at high mental tension and low physical tension.
—Arnold Palmer

CHAPTER NINE

LINKS, COURSES, AND COUNTRY CLUBS

What a beautiful place a golf course is. From the meanest country pasture to the
Pebble Beaches and St. Andrewses of the world, a golf course is to me holy gound.
I feel God in the trees and grass and flowers, in the rabbits and the birds
and the squirrels, in the sky and the water. I feel that I am home.

—Harvey Penick

What really distinguishes golf from other games—more than the
omnipresent awful clothes, the sometimes endless standing around, and the
seeming lack of a human opponent—is the playing field. No two golf courses
are alike, and even the ugliest nine-hole, par-three course is more interesting to
look at than the standard football gridiron, tennis court, or Olympic-sized
swimming pool. What makes certain courses loom large in anyone's conscious-
ness can be fame, nostalgia, comfort, novelty, or merely the matter of opinion.

And that opinion can have dire consequences: Charles Blair Macdonald cut his son-in-law out of his will after the younger man made a disparaging remark about the first hole at the National Golf Links, which Macdonald had designed.

King James VI of Scotland and I of England established the first known golf club organization anywhere, at Blackheath, England, in 1608 (though most of Blackheath's charter members were Scottish). During the reign of George II, around 1750, the first inland courses—technically not "links" but sometimes called so—were laid out near London. Until the 1770s, courses had varying numbers of holes. St. Andrews prior to then featured a dozen holes; after playing the course, golfers then played ten of the same holes in reverse, for a round of 22 holes. When the Royal and Ancient converted its first four holes into two longer ones in 1764, the course round became 18 holes. Since the R & A by then set the standard for all of golf-dom, 18 holes became the accepted number—though many golfers today call the clubhouse bar the "nineteenth hole."

LINKS, COURSES, AND COUNTRY CLUBS

In the United States, the founding of private country clubs came well before the establishment of municipal courses, which were often acts of *noblesse oblige* on the part of the country club establishment. Yet even the earliest private clubs were rudimentary. The Los Angeles Country Club's first course, in 1897, was constructed by sinking nine newly emptied tomato cans at strategic locations on a 16-acre lot. Today it encompasses two 18-hole courses on 325 acres in the center of the city with a land value of $3.2 billion.

At the end of the day when the scorecards are signed, golfers talk about their favorite courses and holes as they might an old love or a heated rival—reliving old rounds just as old soldiers refight their battles. But each is fiercely proud of his or her home course, where the fairways are straighter, the greens are smoother, and the smiles are wider and more plentiful.

The attraction of the game of golf for many club players lies in the simple matter of escape and change—escape from the routine of work and home, and change from the inhibiting environment of factory or office. The attraction of the rolling green acres, the trees, the brooks, the smoothly tailored greens and the warmth of the club and of being part of the club, is compulsive.
—Peter Arliss

A good golf course makes you want to play so badly
you hardly have time to change your shoes.
—Ben Crenshaw

A golf course is something as mysterious as St. Andrews,
as majestic as Pine Valley, as ferocious as Oakmont,
as subtle as Hoylake, as commonplace as Happy Knoll.
—Charles Price

Pine Valley is the shrine of American golf because so many golfers are buried there.
—Ed Sullivan

I say, do you chaps actually try to play this hole
or do you simply photograph it and go on?
—Eustace Storey, member of the British Walker Cup team, to his American
opposition on viewing Pine Valley's punishing Number 2 hole

We think that we shall never see
A tougher course than Pine Valley
Trees and traps wherever we go
And clumps of earth flying through the air
This course was made for you and me
But only God can make a THREE
—Jack McLean and Charlie Yates,
members of the 1936 British and American Walker Cup teams, respectively

To me, the ground here is hallowed. The grass grows greener,
the trees bloom better, there is even warmth to the rocks . . . somehow
or other the sun seems to shine on The Country Club [of Brookline,
Massachusetts] more than any other place I have ever known.
—Francis Ouimet, on the course on which he won the 1913 U.S. Open

Golf in and around Los Angeles tends to be—like the rest
of the landscape—unreal...part Royal and Ancient, part Disneyland.
The Good Ship Lollipop with four-irons.
—Jim Murray

Pebble Beach is built right around my game. Unfortunately, it doesn't touch any part of it.
—Mason Rudolph

No. 9 at Pebble Beach: This hole is harder than trigonometry.
—Hubert Green

No. 11: Probably the worst hole on the course. Then again,
being the worst hole at Pebble [Beach] is like being the ugliest Miss America.
—Rick Reilly

I don't think Pebble Beach will ever be sold to foreign investors. That would be un-American.
—Dave Marr (the course was later sold to Japanese investors)

Crooked Stick Golf Club, site of the 1992 PGA tournament: So long that
figuring distances on some holes, you have to reckon the curvature of the earth.
—David Feherty

At Augusta, history is the biggest thing. There are so many people who
grew up dreaming about winning the Masters. You know you
are going to be immortalized if you win it. It's got more to do with history
and green jackets and azaleas than playing the course.
—Bob Rotella

If you don't get goose bumps when you walk into this place
[Augusta National], you don't have a pulse.
—Hal Sutton

Augusta National is a young man's golf course,
and you really need a young man's nerves to play on it.
—Jack Nicklaus

I'm glad I brought this course, this monster, to its knees.
—Ben Hogan, after winning the 1951 Masters

I've never been to heaven, and thinkin' back on my life, I probably won't
get a chance to go. I guess the Masters is as close as I'm going to get.
—Fuzzy Zoeller, after winning the Masters in 1979

Every good course has a couple of holes where everybody talks
about the tough decisions to make in club selection.
But here [at Augusta National] there are thirteen or fourteen holes like that.
—John Mahaffey

**[Augusta National] is like playing a Salvador Dali
landscape. I expected a clock to fall out
of the trees and hit me in the face.**
—David Feherty

In the minds of many Americans Pinehurst is synonymous with golf.
—William H. Davis

Famous mid-South resorts, including Pinehurst and Southern Pines,
where it is said that there are more golf curses [*sic*]
per square mile than anywhere else in the world. . . .
—North Carolina Tourist Council brochure, late 1950s

There has never been a better example of the sow's-ear-to-silk-purse
metamorphosis than the miracle that James Tuft and Donald Ross wrought in
changing a worthless piece of sandy wasteland in North Carolina into Pinehurst.
—Robert Trent Jones

Robert Trent Jones must have laid out the course in a kennel.
—Bob Rosburg, on the Hazletine National
Golf Club of Chaska, Minnesota, which has ten dog-leg holes

Cypress Point has just completed a highly
successful membership drive: forty players resigned.
—Bob Hope

If Olympic Club were human, it'd be Bela Lugosi. I think it turns into a bat at midnight.
—Jim Murray

Alaska would be an ideal place for courses—
mighty few trees and damn few ladies' foursomes.
—Rex Lardner

A MATTER
OF COURSE

When St. Andrews Golf Club (of Yonkers, New York) founder John Reid sent the Scottish-born U.S. Steel founder Andrew Carnegie a bill for $140 in membership fees in the early 1890s, Carnegie wrote back: "I cannot consider this a proper use of money—no, Sir. I will never be there, and besides, it is a rich club. For the St. Andrew's Society, any-thing—for a swell club, nothing." Carnegie later relented and became a member of the Yonkers country club.

A COURSE OF THEIR OWN

The women's course at the Royal and Ancient Golf Club of St. Andrews, established in 1867, was most likely the first designed expressly for female golfers. American golfer Ruth Underhill dismissed it as "little more than a succession of putting greens." Further, most of the women's courses laid out in Britain the early 1890s, she felt, were "so short that it would seem to us merely an aggravation to play on them, accustomed as we are to the men's long links. Many of the holes are simply approach shots of seventy or eighty yards."

The first American golf clubs to encourage women golfers were Shinnecock Hills (Long Island) in 1891 and Chicago Country Club in 1892. The first USGA women's championship was held at the Meadowbrook Hunt Club in November, 1895. The next year's tournament, at Morris County Golf Club (New Jersey), marked the emergence of Beatrix Hoyt, a sixteen-year-old Shinnecock Hills member who won the title and defended it successfully for the next two years, until being unseated by Underhill in 1899.

This is the great excellence of St. Andrews' links—the artful planting of the
bunkers. Not, of course, that they were planted by any but Nature's hand—
yet one would say with an obvious artistic eye for the golfer's edification.
—Horace G. Hutchinson

St. Andrews never impressed me at all.
I wondered how it got such a reputation.
The only reason could be on account of its age.
—Bill Mehlhorn

St. Andrews? I feel like I'm back visiting an old grandmother.
She's crotchety and eccentric but also elegant.
Anyone who doesn't fall in love with her has no imagination.
—"Champagne" Tony Lema

The reason the Road Hole [Number 17 at St. Andrews]
is the greatest par 4 in the world is because it's a par 5.
—Ben Crenshaw

There's nothing wrong with the St. Andrews course that a hundred
bulldozers couldn't put right. The Old Course needs a dry clean and press.
—Ed Furgol

Until you play it, St. Andrews looks like the sort of real estate you couldn't give away.

—Sam Snead

Essex: It's one of the few courses
I've played that you get a chance to use every club in the bag.
—Johnny Miller

Folks praise the links ayont the Forth—
St. Andrews, Elie, Leven:
About Carnoustie, Dornoch Firth,
Our ears they aft are deavin'.
But Gullane, oh, your wondrous charm
A' other links surpasses;
Inspired we climb your links as once
The ancients climbed Parnassus.
—Traditional Scottish poem

Strangely enough, Turnberry is the only course on the rota
of British Open venues—which consist only of links
courses—where the ocean actually comes into play.
—Greg Norman

**Carnoustie: Moody as Maria Callas,
it rouses to fury when the westerlies come roaring
out of the Atlantic across the width of Scotland.**
—Fred Tupper

Carnoustie Golf Club, Scotland: A good swamp, spoiled.
—Gary Player

**Anyone who criticizes a golf course is like a person
invited to a house for dinner who, on leaving,
tells the host that the food was lousy.**
—Gary Player

Some players would complain if they
were playing on Dolly Parton's bedspread.
—Jimmy Demaret

**People may grumble about a course being difficult,
but they always come back to it the next day.**
—W. Herbert Fowler

CHAPTER TEN

THE CHAMPIONS

What does it take to be a champion?

Desire, dedication, determination, concentration and the will to win.

—Patty Berg

Although the first international foursome match, between England and Scotland, was held on the Links of Leith in 1682, the first golf tournament of any consequence was the British Open, which was first held at Prestwick, Scotland in 1860. While only eleven players participated, the "gallery" of spectators as it was termed by one journalist (after the cheap seats in theatres), comprised a cross section of British society, mingling as equals for the first time. They quickly found and followed their favorite players, and the admiration of the most gifted and charismatic golfers has continued unabated from that day forward.

Some said the Open was founded in order to determine a successor to the man who was known simply as "the champion," Allan Robertson, who died the year before. Robertson had been the first golfer to break 80 at St. Andrews, and the first real golf professional. Tom Morris, Sr. was Robertson's apprentice at St. Andrews, and his playing partner in many matches. "Old Tom" won four British Opens, but was eclipsed by his son "Young Tom," who won his first Open at 17 and his fourth in 1871 just before his death at 24, making him the greatest golfer in Scotland and, hence, the world.

English dominance of the game took over in 1890 when John Ball from Liverpool became the first of his countrymen (and the first amateur) to win the Open. His eight British Amateur championships remain a record total for any major tournament in history. "The Triumvirate," James Braid, J.H. Taylor, and Harry Vardon dominated golf in the early part of the 20th century, with sixteen British Open titles among them. Vardon, a six-time Open champ, frequently toured America, and is credited with popularizing the game and introducing the overlapping "Vardon Grip." The Americans claimed supremacy in golf when 20-year-old ex-caddy Francis Ouimet beat Vardon for the 1913 U.S. Open Championship. Ouimet was well-liked in Britain and became the first American to be named Captain of the Royal and Ancient Golf Club at St. Andrews.

In the 1920s, with eleven major championships and an elegant lifestyle, Walter Hagen was the first professional golfer as opposed to a golf professional. As popular as Babe Ruth, Jack Dempsey, and Red Grange in a golden age of sports heroes, "The Haig" refused to sell equipment or repair golf clubs (although he was happily paid to endorse both), preferring to bank on his ability as a player. Almost single-handedly, Hagen advanced the social standing of golf pro from servant to celebrity, even playing golf with King Edward VIII of England, whom he called "Eddie."

Bobby Jones remains the quintessential American golfing legend. Robert Tyre Jones, Jr. won all of his 13 major championships as an amateur before the age of 28, including the first Grand Slam (then the two major Amateurs, British and U.S., and the U.S. and British Opens in the same year) in 1930. After his retirement from competition, he went on to film his classic golf lessons and establish Augusta National and the Masters tournament. In the 1930s, Gene Sarazen was the first player to win all four modern majors—the U.S. and British Opens, the PGA, and the Masters—a feat since equalled only by Ben Hogan, Gary Player, and Jack Nicklaus, who also broke Jones's record of 13 majors.

Two women, one British and one American, achieved equal celebrity with their male counterparts in the 1920s and 30s. Joyce Wethered, Lady Heathcoat-Amory, was the first great woman golfer; starting in 1920, she was English Ladies champion for five straight years, and she won four British women's championships in six attempts. Her stylish, graceful golf swing was often compared to that of Bobby Jones. Glenna Collett (later Vare) was six times U.S. women's champion over a period of 14 years, twice runner-up, and twice a semi-finalist.

Byron Nelson won the U.S. Open, PGA, and Masters before World War II, beating out fellow legends Ben Hogan and Sam Snead. In 1945, "Lord Byron" won eleven straight PGA tournaments. Snead won three Masters, three PGA championships, and a British Open among his 84 official PGA tour titles. He is the only golfer to have shot his age on the PGA tour—a record likely to stand since the advent of the Senior Tour. Hogan practiced more, hit longer, and placed better shots than any other golfer of his generation.

Mary Kathryn (Mickey) Wright ruled the LPGA tour in the early 1960s, winning four LPGA championships and four U.S. Women's Opens. "The Big Three" among men in the 1960s were Arnold Palmer, Gary Player, and Jack

Nicklaus. "Arnie's Army" followed their hero's slashing, dashing style across a course, as golf became a popular televised spectator sport. The South African Player was a world-class golfer who won tournaments on every continent where golf is played, and has been the most successful non-American on both the PGA and Senior tours. Nicklaus, "the Golden Bear," has the best majors record in golfing history: a record six Masters, four U.S. Opens, three British Opens, and five PGA championships. Nicklaus reigned over the golf world until Tom Watson took over with his streak of eight major wins in the 1970s and 1980s.

In recent years, as golf has spread across boundaries both territorial and economic, the game has gone global and the faces of the major champions themselves have changed. On today's leader-boards Spaniard Seve Ballesteros, Australian Greg Norman, South African Ernie Els, and German Berhard Langer vie against a new generation of American golfers led by Masters champion Tiger Woods and British Open champion Justin Leonard, both in professional tournaments and in international team competitions such as the Ryder Cup, which pits the best American professionals against the best pros from the countries of the European Union.

Winners are a different breed of cat. They have an inner drive
and are willing to give of themselves whatever it takes to win.
—Byron Nelson

Once the fundamentals of golf are mastered, about ninety percent
of the game depends on judgment and attitude.
On the pro tournament level, I'm inclined to raise the figure to 95 percent.
—Arnold Palmer

I don't think people appreciate how hard we work, and mentally how hard it is to win a major.
—Nick Faldo

Winners learn to accept the swing they bring to the golf course on any given
day and to score with it. They win tournaments, as often as not,
because they use their short game and their mind to avoid a high round
on the day or days when their swing is not what they wanted.
If they need to work on their mechanics, they do it after the round is over,
or they take a week off and go to the practice tee.
—Bob Rotella

The players themselves can be classified into two groups: the attractions and the entry fees.
—Jimmy Demaret

It's really hard when people are telling you how good you should be all the time; it's really hard to live up to everybody else's expectations.
—Hal Sutton

No tournament owes me anything. I have to go out and earn it.
—Colin Montgomerie

The mark of a champion is the ability to make the most of good luck and the best of bad.
—20th-century American adage

Give me a wind and I'll show you who'll be champion.
—Ben Sayers

It is impossible to outplay an opponent you can't out-think.
—Lawson Little

If you keep shooting par at them, they all crack sooner or later.
—Bobby Jones

Tournaments are won on Sunday and on the back nine.
—Jack Nicklaus

To play well on the final holes of a major championship,
you need a certain arrogance. You have to find a trance,
some kind of self-hypnosis that's almost a state of grace.
—Hale Irwin

Just to play in [the British Open] is great. To do well in it is fantastic. To win it is a dream.
—Ian Baker-Finch, after winning the British Open in 1991

Playing the U.S. Open is like tippy-toeing through hell.
—Jerry McGee

Golf, especially championship golf, isn't supposed to be any fun,
was never meant to be fair, and never will make any sense.
—Charles Price

I don't care what anybody says.
The first tournament is not the hardest one to win.
It's always the second one.
—John Daly

Like a hurricane [John Daly's] arrival came without warning
and his game spells danger wherever he plays.
—David Leadbetter

An amateur golfer is one who plays for honor.
In my mind, that's tougher than playing for money.
—Willie Turnsea

The only stats I care about are paychecks and victories.
—Greg Norman

Every kid learning how to play golf dreams about winning the Masters,
about winning the Open, not about being the leading money winner.
I've never shortchanged myself on dreams.
—Tom Kite

**Victory is everything. You can spend the money,
but you can never spend the memories.**
—Ken Venturi

Walter Hagen was the first player I knew that earned $1 million from golf,
and of course he spent it, too.
Sam Snead earned $1 million, too—and he saved $2 million.
—Fred Corcoran

Making a million or having the return of his laundry delayed by fiscal factors,
nothing bothers [Walter] Hagen; he could relax sitting on a hot stove.
—Tommy Armour

A VICTORY OF
DUBIOUS DISTINCTION

Glenna Collett Vare had won six national championships and become a player of international stature by the time she entered her first and only Philadelphia Country Club ladies' championship tournament in the late 1930s. The club was so honored by her entry and so sure that she would win that they ordered a grand new silver trophy from the venerable local jewelry firm of Bailey, Banks and Biddle. The jewelers promised that the prize would be delivered to the club before the final match.

Vare was several holes ahead by the seventh hole of the final round, and the trophy still had not been delivered. By the fourteenth hole, she was so far ahead that the match would be over quickly—and, despite several phone calls to Bailey Banks, without a trophy in hand. Desperate, the chairman of the golf committee raced home and grabbed a large trophy one of his show dogs had won, quickly polished it, and presented it to Vare near the eighteenth green, intending to explain all to her later. After thanking the chairman, Glenna looked at the silver bowl, dropped it back on the table and departed angrily. Only then did the chairman look at the inscription on his dog's award: "Best Bitch in Show."

I envy that man [Miller Barber], because he makes
a hundred thousand dollars a year like I do, but nobody knows him.
—Mickey Mantle

If we all played golf like Mac Smith, the National Open Championship
could be played on one course every day in the year
and never a divot mark would scar the beautiful fairway.
He treats the grass of a golf course as though it were an altar cloth.
—Tommy Armour

If you can't outplay them, outwork them.
—Ben Hogan

I'm only scared of three things: lightning, a side-hill putt, and Ben Hogan.
—Sam Snead

It's not whether you win or lose, but whether I win or lose.
—Sandy Lyle

Winning has always meant much to me,
but winning friends has meant the most.
—Babe Didrikson Zaharias

She made women's golf. She put the hit in the swing.
—Patty Berg, describing Babe Didrikson Zaharias

You'd think I'd never done anything else but hit that shot [which won the Masters in 1935]. In the Orient for a while I became known as Mr. Double Eagle, which non-golfers probably took to mean that I was an Indian chief.
—Gene Sarazen

The better you putt, the bolder you play.
—Don January

Don January's playing with all the passion and verve of a meter reader.
—Vin Scully

Palmer and Player played superbly, but Nicklaus
played a game with which I am not familiar.
—Bobby Jones

I'll be honest about it: I want to win more than [Bobby] Jones.
That's what you play for, to separate yourself from the crowd.
—Jack Nicklaus

[Jack Nicklaus] is the only golfer who has become a legend in his spare time.
—Chi Chi Rodriguez

Mickey [Wright] set standards of achievement that have not been surpassed, the most lasting contribution any player can give to their game, especially when, as with Mickey Wright, it is gracefully borne.
—Pat Ward-Thomas

[Judy Rankin] is so small, she might get lost in an unreplaced divot.
—Bob Toski (who himself was only 5'7" and 130 pounds)

A smart fella once told me that a fine golfer only has one thing, and that's his fine golf—and that if he forgets it, he's a fool. Tom Watson never forgets.
—Byron Nelson

I have never felt so lonely as on a golf course in the midst of a championship with thousands of people around.
—Bobby Jones

To me, the gallery becomes nothing but a wall. I don't even see their faces.
—Lanny Wadkins

Part of my philosophy is that a gallery, far from upsetting me, psyches me up.
—Nancy Lopez

I grew up watching Betsy King, Patty Sheehan, Nancy Lopez.
They were all my role models, and here I am playing against them, and once
in a while beating them. It's a nice feeling, but it's also hard to believe.
—Annika Sorenstam

Great champions learn from past experiences, whether those be good or bad.
A lot of times a guy needs to be knocked down before he gets up and fights.
—Paul Azinger

Paul Azinger is a true inspiration to all golfers.
He plays with his heart as well as his mind. If Norman Rockwell had
painted a family man/golfer, he would have done a portrait of Paul.
—Dave Stockton

People are always telling me I should do one thing or another. I should change
my grip or shorten my swing. I should practice more and goof around less.
I shouldn't smile on Sunday . . . I should . . . I shouldn't . . .
Frankly I don't know why they worry. It's my life—and I don't worry.
—Fred Couples

If [Laura Davies] used a driver off the tee and kept it in the fairway, the rest of us would be playing for second most of the time.
—Nancy Lopez

[Corey Pavin] plays the game of golf as if he has a plane to catch—
as if he were double-parked and left the meter running.
Guys move slower leaving hotel fires.
—Jim Murray

**The biggest thing is to have the mind-set and
the belief you can win every tournament going in.
A lot of guys don't have that. Nicklaus had it. . . .
He felt he was going to beat everybody.**
—Tiger Woods

Tiger Woods has done tremendous things for golf overall.
He's very impressive. I learn a lot by watching him play.
—Annika Sorenstam

It's flattering to hear people compare us; it doesn't bother me one bit.
Our careers have paralleled, but it's hard to compare us
because Tiger is the new version of Arnold Palmer.
He revolutionized golf and Tiger's doing it in a new way.
—Kelli Kuehne

I thought it was a new golf course.
—Sandy Lyle, when asked about the then-promising amateur, Tiger Woods

CHAPTER ELEVEN

THE LITERARY GOLFER

Golf's lexicon of colorful words and phrases is its crowning achievement.

For long after the urge of the ability to play the game leaves us,

golf's joyful adjectives and modifiers, its splendid superlatives

and unequalled accolades ring in my ear the waves of a familiar ocean.

—Robert H. K. Browning

The author as golfer or keen observer of the game is a tradition that goes back at least to the 1600s. In the 17th century, Samuel Pepys, the diarist, seems to have been the first writer of note to comment on golf; he at least played the game, unlike Dr. Samuel Johnson, who in the 18th century wrote of the game from a disdainful distance, not as a player himself. The Romantic poet William Wordsworth had taken the game up in his Lake District boyhood, and wrote rhapsodically of "a day spent in strenuous idleness." Hundreds of literary golfers have followed in his footsteps, many devoting virtually all of their professional lives to writing passionately about the sublime pleasures—and agonizing pains—of the game.

In the past hundred years, the best golf writing has been American. In 1897, Midwestern humorist George Ade offered the proof that golf had arrived in the United States: he satirized it. In Ade's *Golf in Four Acts*, an "outline" for a play, a hero, a heroine, and a villain are lost for days in a "vast wilderness" playing a single game of golf.

The greatest American golf writer was Herbert Warren Wind, a *New Yorker* profiler who produced the classic books *The Complete Golfer* and *The Story of American Golf*, and collaborated with Gene Sarazen and Jack Nicklaus for their autobiographies, and with Ben Hogan on *The Modern Fundamentals of Golf*. Many other golfing greats, such as Walter Hagen and Bobby Jones, have proved to be equally adept at writing about the game they have so elegantly mastered.

In recent years, novelists such as John Updike, non-fiction writers such as George Plimpton (*The Bogey Man*), and humorists such as Bob Hope (*Confessions of a Hooker*) have been their most eloquent when writing about golf. More than sixty magazines have golf as their sole subject, and the World Wide Web contains more and better websites devoted to golf than any other game.

It seems that the most reticent of men on other subjects
no sooner takes to golf than eloquence descends upon him.
—John Hogben

The sport's best medium
is not television, radio or the eye.
Even more than baseball [golf's] the sport of words.
—Thomas Boswell

The smaller the ball used in the sport, the better the book.
There are superb books about golf, very good books about baseball,
not very many good books about basketball, and no good books on beachballs.
—George Plimpton

This all our life we frolik and gay,
And instead of court revels we merrily play,
At Trap, at Rules, and at Barley-break run,
At Goff and at Foot-Ball, and when we have done,
These innocent sports, we'll laugh and lie down.
—Thomas Shadwell

The average player would rather play than watch. Those who don't play
can't possibly appreciate the subtleties of the game. Trying to get their
attention with golf is like selling Shakespeare in the neighborhood saloon.
—Bob Toski

A GOLFER'S SHAKESPEARE

Horace G. Hutchinson wrote, "Human nature is so funny; it is a thousand pities that neither Aristotle nor Shakespeare was a golfer. There is no other game that strips the soul so naked." Although the Bard of Avon didn't actually play or literally write about golf, he could easily have been doing so when he penned these inspired excerpts from his plays:

I'll call for clubs.
—Henry VI, Part II

Put up your iron.
—Twelfth Night

He is not so big as the end of his club.
—Love's Labours Lost

But make you ready your stiff bats and clubs.
—Coriolanus

What subtle hole is this, whose mouth
is covered with rude-growing briers?
—Titus Andronicus

Cursed be the hand that made these fatal holes!
—*Richard III*

By thy approach thou makest me most unhappy.
—*Two Gentlemen of Verona*

In your bad strokes,
Brutus, you give good words.
—*Julius Caesar*

Here's that shall drive some of them to a noncome.
—*Much Ado About Nothing*

Why, these balls bound!
—*All's Well That Ends Well*

He knows the game.
How true he keeps the wind.
—*Henry VI, Part III*

We have done our course;
there's money for your pains.
—*Othello*

It is impossible to imagine Goethe or Beethoven being good at billiards or golf.

—H. L. Mencken

The humor of golf is a divine comedy in the deepest sense.
Like all sources of laughter it lies in contrast and paradox;
in the thought of otherwise grave men gravely
devoting hours and money to a technique which so often they,
apparently alone, do not know they can never master.
The solemnity of their eternal failure is vastly comic.
The perpetualness of their hope is nobly humorous.

—R.C. Robertson-Glasgow

I once thought of becoming a political cartoonist because they only have
to come up with one idea a day. Then I thought I'd become
a sportswriter instead, because they don't have to come up with any.

—Sam Snead

The professional golf watcher never catches the action.
I could write a volume on *Great Moments in Golf I Have Missed.*

—Peter Dobereiner

Years ago we discovered the exact point, the dead center of middle age.
It occurs when you are too young to take up golf and too old to rush the net.

—Franklin P. Adams

To that man, age brought only golf instead of wisdom.
—George Bernard Shaw

Golf is a way of claiming the privileges of age and retaining the playthings of childhood.
—Samuel Johnson

One particular set of golfers, the youngest of whom was turned
of four-score . . . were all gentlemen of independent fortunes who had amused
themselves with this pastime for the best part of a century without ever
having felt the least alarm from sickness or disgust; and they never went to bed
without having each the best part of a gallon of claret in his belly.
Such uninterrupted exercise, cooperating with the keen air from the sea,
must, without all doubt, keep the appetite always on edge,
and steel the constitution against all the common attacks of distemper.
—Tobias Smollett

Golf is a game whose aim is to put a very small ball into an even smaller
hole with instruments singularly ill-adapted to the purpose
—Lewis Carroll (also attributed to Winston Churchill and Woodrow Wilson)

Golf is a good walk spoiled.
—Mark Twain

Golf is a lot of walking,
broken up by disappointment and bad arithmetic.
—Earl Wilson

I regard golf as an expensive way of playing marbles.
—G. K. Chesterton

Golf is an open exhibition of overweening ambition,
courage deflated by stupidity, skill soured by a whiff of arrogance. . . .
These humiliations are the essence of the game.
—Alistair Cooke

Golf is a choke game. Nobody ever shanked a three-iron because
his opponent threw him a curve or put too much topspin on the ball.
When Scott Hoch missed a three-foot putt to blow the 1989
Masters, the ball was sitting perfectly still when he hit it and the crowd
was perfectly silent. It was completely, entirely, totally him.
That's why golf is also the cruelest game.
—Mark Mulvoy

Yes, it is a cruel game, one in which the primitive instincts of man
are given full play, and the difference between golf and fisticuffs is that
in one the pain is of the mind and in the other it is of the body.
—Henry Leach

Golf combines two favorite American pastimes:
taking long walks and hitting things with a stick.
—P. J. O'Rourke

One of the hardest things about becoming a golfer, for me, has been finding
a way to conceive of the game as something more than a pastime
for people who have more leisure than they deserve. For an American
of a certain age, cultural outlook and political inclination, a love of golf is more
than faintly embarrassing. Is there any sound more evocative of grody
Republican smugness than the sound of golf spikes on brick?
—David Owen

PAR FOR THE COURSE, FOR A SATIRIST

One afternoon at Burning Tree, President Warren G. Harding played with sportswriter Grantland Rice and humorist Ring Lardner, who occasionally wrote about golf. Harding, a restless type, had the rude habit of walking ahead of his competitors after he had made his tee shot. Driving ahead of Lardner, the President sauntered down the fairway and stood next to a dead apple tree on the left. Lardner sliced somewhat and hit the tree, causing a branch to break and drop onto Harding's shoulder. The President, unhurt, waited for Lardner to join him and offer an apology. Instead, Lardner cracked, "I did all I could to make Coolidge President." Harding laughed so hard he dropped his club.

After nine holes, the Secret Service man keeping score reported that Rice was ahead of Harding, 44 to 55. On hearing the news, Lardner, maintaining his irreverent tone, snapped back, "I'd rather be Rice than President."

If you thought about merely walking down the street the way you think about golf you'd wind up falling off the curb. Yet a good straight drive or a soft chip stiff to the pin gives him the bliss that used to come thinking of women, imagining if only you and she were alone on some desert island.

—John Updike

On the average, a maximum of 4.097 percent of the time associated with a round of golf is spent whacking the golf ball with a golf club.

—Geoff Howson

The uglier a man's legs are, the better he plays golf.

—H. G. Wells

Golf is a wonderful exercise.
You can stand on your feet for hours and watch somebody else putt.

—Will Rogers

The least thing upset him on the links. He missed short putts because of the uproar of the butterflies in the adjoining meadows.

—P. G Wodehouse

A match at golf this day with Cozen Roger, and should have greatly beaten him but for what he said to me as we walked to the 15th tee, being by this time 2 up. When he asks me: "By the way, Sam, what is all this to do 'twixt you and your Mrs.?" Which puts me in a pretty twitter as to what he said and what I shall best say to him, so that I did most vilely foozle my drive, and thereafter not a stroke could I strike clean.

—Samuel Pepys

A golf course is the epitome of all that is purely transitory in the universe, a space not to dwell in, but to get over as quickly as possible.

—Jean Giradoux

At Jinja there is both hotel and golf course. The latter is, I believe, the only course in the world which posts a special rule that the player may remove his ball from hippopotamus footprints.

—Evelyn Waugh

If you want them to play your course, don't put rocks on the green.

—Terry Southern

A man may be the best player and still he cannot win the championship unless the luck be with him.

—Bernard Darwin

Golf is so popular simply because it is the best
game in the world at which to be bad. . . . At golf
it is the bad player who gets the most strokes.
—A. A. Milne

I won't try to describe A.R.'s game, beyond saying the way
he played it would have taken him three years of solid practice
to work up to where he could be called a duffer.
—Paul Gallico

I like golf because you can be really terrible
at it and not look much dorkier than anybody else.
—Dave Barry

The supergolfer has style and hence is called a stylist. The golfer has
form, but is not hence called a formist. For some reason this
word has not yet been invented. But the subgolfer has neither form nor
style and is never called much of anything worth repeating.
Yet let it be said at once that we are the only class of golfers of any real
importance to the game. We are its spine and its sinews, comprising
ninety-two percent of its players. Lacking us the supergolfer could
not play his tournaments nor be photographed for *Golf, Pastry and Plumbing*.
—Harry Leon Wilson

CHAPTER TWELVE

QUIPS ON EQUIPMENT

Perhaps the most important thing I can tell you

about equipment is to experiment and keep an open mind.

—Gary Player

From feather-stuffed leather balls and baffy cleek clubs, to aerodynamically designed hot pink dimpled balls and persimmon woods with titanium shafts and beryllium copper clubheads, the evolution of golfing gear has chronicled players' obsessions with finding the perfect tools for the perfect round. The quest for the Holy Grail is nothing compared to the search for the perfect putter, not to mention the precisely optimal dodecahedron dimple pattern on a golf ball.

In golf's early days, both balls and clubs were made of wood. "Featheries," balls concocted from a bowler hatful of chicken feathers boiled and stuffed into a cowhide covering, represented the first major equipment advance in the 1500s. Although they often had to be reboiled and reshaped, featheries allowed lofty drives as long as 300 yards, and remained the only sort of golf ball for three hundred years. By 1848, the introduction of "gutties," balls made of the rubbery Malayan tree sap gutta-percha, revolutionized the game. Gutties needed less boiling and reshaping, cost less and lasted longer, and, most importantly, offered much better flights and farther drives. The introduction of the gutty remains the greatest innovation in golf history, having fostered the expansion and lengthening of existing courses and the development of new ones. The total takeover by gutta-percha balls induced legions of new players to start playing the game, and challenged clubmakers to further refine their craft.

In 1899, a Cleveland businessman, Coburn Haskell, invented the rubber-cored wound ball that, with slight modifications such as balata coverings, remains the golfing standard. The Haskell ball, which was marketed by B. F. Goodrich, got its first big boost when Walter Travis used it to win the 1901 United States Amateur Championship. By 1903 the Haskell ball's acceptance was so universal that the named appeared lower-cased and its inventor became extremely wealthy. Again, the new ball soared farther than its predecessor, and golf courses had to be expanded. The British ball and club maker William

Taylor introduced the dimple pattern in 1908, applying the same aerodynamic principle that caused the Wright Brothers' airplane to fly—the indentations on the ball trap air, causing it to move faster over the top of the ball than around the bottom, making the ball rise.

Innovations in club-making have been more gradual and less dramatic. For centuries, each golf club was handmade, individually bought, and handed down to succeeding generations. The earliest clubs, called brassies, spoons, cleeks, and niblicks, were hickory-shafted with heads of briar and hedgethorne, sometimes fortified with pieces of bone and metal. Iron clubheads arrived in the middle 1600s. Two hundred years after that, driving irons, putters, and bunker niblicks (today's sand wedges) became staples of most golfbags. The Industrial Revolution and the universal adoption of the gutty ball inspired a new era of clubmakers, now drop-forging their irons though still hand-carving their woods. By the time golf took hold in the United States, around 1890, golf clubs had been regularized for a quarter of a century. Steel shafts replaced wood by the late 1920s, and in 1930 the matched set of numbered clubs was introduced—a successful marketing ploy that has since become a standard.

Today's persimmon woods, graphite shafts, and outsized clubheads are arguably more wishful thinking than real innovation: graphite shafts add only two or three yards to a drive, and evidence that increased clubhead size yields a larger "sweet spot" is strictly anecdotal.

Golfers also love to spend their money on non-essential garb and gadgets, from lambskin left gloves to video swing analyzers. From the turn of the century through the 1930s, special golfing knickers called "plus-fours" went in and out of fashion every few years (the name derived from clothing makers adding four inches to the standard knee-length baseball knickers to create a blousing effect), and are still worn on the PGA tour by Payne Stewart. Golf carts, since their introduction as gas-powered converted ice cream trucklets in the mid-1950s, have all but replaced caddies—most probably because the carts can't criticize or count.

[Golf is] a game in which a ball one-and-a-half inches in diameter
is placed on a ball eight thousand miles in diameter.
The object is to hit the small ball but not the large.
—John Cunningham

[The golf ball] is white, dimpled like a bishop's knees, and is the size of small mandarin oranges or those huge pills which vets blow down the throats of constipated cart-horses.
—Frank Muir

One of the advantages bowling has over golf
is that you very seldom lose a bowling ball.
—Don Carter

You can't lose an old golf ball.
—John Willis

No power on earth will deter men from using
a ball that will add to the length of their drive.
—*Golf Illustrated*, describing the advent of the Haskell ball

The advent of the rubber ball was instrumental in creating an entirely different method of striking the object. The solid ball required to be hit for carry, whereas it was quickly apparent that the Haskell ball lent itself to an enormous run. I hold the firm opinion that from this date the essential attitude toward accuracy was completely lost sight of. This was the start of the craze for length and still more length.

—Harry Vardon

The wretched Haskell ball appeared and upset all our calculations about golf courses. Our little 18 hole course [The Country Club at Brookline, Massachusetts] was ruined by it.

—G. Herbert Windeler, then USGA President, describing the rubber-cored ball's effect on the game

I have talked to golf balls all my golfing life. I accept that a golf ball is inanimate; I understand that a golf ball does not have ears or a brain or even a nervous system. But it is, nonetheless, pleasing to see a golf ball pop right out of a bunker at the exact moment you've yelled, "Skip, golf ball, skip!" So, yes, I talk to golf balls; I admit to that. If I had to guess, I'd say we talkers are in the majority.

—Michael Bamberger

"Great Scot, ye've holed in one!"
"Aye, it saves, the wear and tear o' the ball."

—Traditional Scottish joke

I don't like number 4 balls. And I don't like fives, sixes or sevens on my cards.
—George Archer

Golf bag: a bulky container of paradoxical weight properties—one
is too heavy for a 200-pound adult male seeking exercise;
two are considered the correct burden for a 120-pound child.
—C. P. Donnel, Jr.

Golf is great exercise, particularly climbing in and out of the carts.
—Jack Berry

A man ought to have a doctor's prescription to be allowed to use a golf cart.
—Dr. Paul Dudley White, while he was personal physician of President Eisenhower

Showing up at a golf course as an adult with your own clubs
is like showing up for a final exam.
It's assumed you know something about the subject.
—John Powers

It isn't really a game; it's an art. If it were a game, played at unreflective speed,
such as hockey, you would use one club only. Most golfers carry fourteen
for the same reason that a painter's easel can accommodate
fourteen or more brushes: they are not too many for the delicate, varied
and agonizedly solitary and introspective making of strokes.
—Peter Black

The club weighs less than a pound. The ball weighs less than two ounces.
We don't need to prepare for violence.
—Bob Toski

When you have a fight with a club, the club always wins.
—Patty Hayes

The most exquisitely satisfying act in the world of golf is that
of throwing a club. The full backswing, the delayed wrist action,
the flowing follow-through, followed by that unique whirring sound,
reminiscent only of a passing flock of starlings, are without parallel in sport.
—Henry Longhurst

Longer clubs won't help a tall golfer.
—Jack Nicklaus

You've got to learn to have a relationship with the club head,
to know where it's going and what it's doing, and how it's positioned
throughout the swing. But most of all, you've got to feel the club.
—Jim Flick

It doesn't much matter what kind of a clubhead
is on one end of that shiny metal shaft if a fat head is on the other.
—Robinson Murray

For most amateurs,
the best wood in the bag is the pencil.
—Chi Chi Rodriguez

If you hit a ball with a mashie, it will sometimes
go further than if you miss it with a driver.
—Ring Lardner

No just and merciful God would demand as the price of salvation
that we all learn to hit a one-iron.
—Charles P. Pierce

In case you don't know very much about the game of golf,
a good one-iron shot is about as easy to come by as an understanding wife.
—Dan Jenkins

The one-iron is almost unplayable. You keep it in your bag the way
you keep a Dostoyevsky novel in your bookcase—with the vague notion
that you will try it some day. In the meantime, it impresses your friends.
—Tom Scott and Geoffrey Cousins

Actually, the only time I ever took out a one-iron was to kill a tarantula.
And it took a seven to do that.
—Jim Murray

**The niblick, with its heavy head of iron,
is a capital club for knocking down solicitors.**
—19th-century English saying

I call my sand wedge my half-Nelson,
because I can always strangle the opposition with it.
—Byron Nelson

It's still embarrassing. I asked my caddie for a sand wedge,
and ten minutes later he came back with a ham on rye.
—Chi Chi Rodriguez, on his long-standing accent problems

The less said about the putter the better. Here is an instrument of torture,
designed by Tantalus and forged in the devil's own smithy.
—"Champagne" Tony Lema

**I may be the only golfer never to have broken
a single putter, if you don't count the one I twisted
into a loop and threw into a bush.**
—Thomas Boswell

Tommy Bolt's putter has spent more time in the air than Lindbergh.
—Jimmy Demaret

SARTORIAL EQUIPMENT

For golf, clothing has been important—and brightly colored—since the beginning. Early Scot players wore orange-colored jackets above their kilts much as hunters have always worn red, so as not to be mistaken for animals or hit by golf balls. Traditionally, women were expected to wear the heavy raiment of their Sunday best; only with the age of the flapper in the 1920s were they liberated from constricting clothing on the golf course and allowed to wear short skirts and short sleeves, and eventually slacks (although to this day some clubs prohibit women in pants). At one particularly stuffy English club in 1927, the Clubhouse Rules Committee was still insisting on two-tiered dresses for women on the course; since the committee was made up of older men with younger wives, the latter went on strike and withheld conjugal relations until the rule was rescinded two months later. The new regulation, however, read even more ridiculously: "Trousers may be worn by women on the course, but must be taken off upon entering the clubhouse."

Ironically, men from the early 1900s through the 1930s tended to dress like conservative businessmen while playing golf, complete with neckties and jackets— although flat caps and "plus-fours" provided a specifically golfing fashion statement. In the 1940s, Jimmy Demaret, the Texan who was the first player to win three Masters titles re-introduced wild colors to golf shirts and trousers while his competitors were still in white shirts and grey or brown slacks. Golfing attire has continued to reach new levels of outlandishness ever since; as the American comedian Robin Williams has said, "Golf is the only game in which middle-class, middle-aged guys can dress like pimps."

To be a true artist on the greens, you should be as selective
in choosing a putter as, say, a master violinist would
be in choosing his or her instrument.
—Paul Runyan

It's a marriage. If I had to choose between my wife and my putter . . . well, I'd miss her.
—Gary Player

Baffling late-life discovery: Golfers wear those awful clothes on purpose.
—Herb Caen

Emmett Kelly picks out his clothes . . . Doug [Sanders] looks
like he took a bad trip through a paint factory.
—Don Rickles

There is one more important characteristic: it must have a large and smooth area for advertising material. That, above all, is the purpose of golf hats.
—Peter Dobereiner

Knickers are good for my golf game.
They're cooler in hot weather because the air circulates in them
and they're warmer in cold weather because they trap the body heat.
—Payne Stewart

Claude Harmon not only taught me most of what I know
about the golf swing, he took me out of Argyle socks.
—Dave Marr

I thought all the guys who played golf
[in high school] were a bunch of sissies.
They all wore pink sweaters.
—Larry Nelson, who played football and basketball in high school

People who wear white shoes are either golfers or tourists.
—Jimmy Cannon

I feel calm in calm colors. I don't want people to watch the way I dress.
I want people to watch the way I play.
—Seve Ballesteros

....

CHAPTER THIRTEEN

GOLF AND ENTERTAINMENT

Give me golf clubs, the fresh air and a beautiful partner

and you can keep my golf clubs and the fresh air.

—Jack Benny

The human drama and divine comedy of the golf course have long lured professional entertainers to the game. The legendary 18th-century British stage actor David Garrick was the first famous performer to take up golf, in large part because he had most afternoons off while working in repertory. In 1906, Reginald Bacchus, in an article in *Fry's Journal* entitled "Stage and Athletics," credited the game with "lifting touring theatrical players from a decadent life of late nights spent in pubs (or worse) to the healthful and moral life of a golfer— fresh-faced, athletic and honourable. [While playing golf] the actor meets doctors, lawyers and merchants, and learns to be a much nicer man, a much more useful citizen, and . . . a much better actor."

American entertainers took up golf in a major way in the late 1910s and 1920s, when the movie colony moved permanently to Southern California, where they could play the game year-round between pictures. "America's Sweetheart," Mary Pickford, and her athletic husband Douglas Fairbanks led the silent film colony's enthusiastic coterie of golfers, playing several times a week themselves and donating money for regional tournament prizes. In 1930, Pickford's next husband, Buddy Rogers, was typecast as a young golfer in the first screen musical about the game, *Follow Thru*, in which he and Nancy Carroll sang the hit "We're a Peach of a Pair." Although half of Hollywood seems to have played golf year-round for nine decades, there have been precious few golfing movies. But from the 1930s series of comic shorts about golf featuring W. C. Fields (who was himself an accomplished player), to Kevin Costner's portrayal of a seedy pro in *Tin Cup* in 1996, most of them have been hits. Only Ben Hogan among professionals has been the subject of a feature "biopic," 1951's *Follow the Sun* starring Glenn Ford, although Susan Clark won an Emmy as Babe Didrikson Zaharias in the exemplary 1975 television movie *Babe*.

The two best-known 20th-century golfing entertainers are Bob Hope and Bing Crosby, who met on the same vaudeville bill at New York's Capitol Theatre and first began playing the game together in 1932. When Hope moved West to make movies, he built his home on Lakeside Country Club in the Toluca Lake section of Los Angeles. He also constructed a second home in Palm Springs, where he has presided over the Bob Hope Desert Classic, a professional/celebrity charity tournament, for more than forty years. As recently as three months before his 93rd birthday, Hope teed off with Ronald Reagan, another ex-performer, at The Los Angeles Country Club, on the former President's 85th birthday.

The most famous female golfing entertainer was the singer Dinah Shore, who had one of the four official LPGA major tournaments named for her; it is held annually in the Palm Springs area. Jack Lemmon is the most ardent, terrible celebrity golfer, with an official handicap of 20, but more like a 36, according to most observers. Country star Vince Gill is a "scratch" golfer, while James Garner is a six handicap, Jack Nicholson a 12, Sean Connery a 17, and rocker Eddie Van Halen a 19.

The thing I've noticed most is that celebrities aren't celebrities
on the golf course. They're more relaxed. They don't have to play a role.

—Mac Hunter, on the celebrity members of Riviera Country Club in Los Angeles,
where he is Head Professional

Golf is ridiculous with actors. I've lost my best friend to golf. They sit
around going, "Golf, golf, golf." I lived next to a golf course in New Jersey
as a kid and caddied from twelve to nineteen, so I can't stand golf.

—Tate Donovan

I would rather play Hamlet on Broadway with no rehearsal than tee off at Pebble Beach on television.

—Jack Lemmon

Jack Lemmon has been in more bunkers than Eva Braun.

—Phil Harris

Golf is not a creative game. A creative actor will reach
the top of his profession. So will a creative basketball player.
But a golfer whose mind is creative won't make it.

—Craig T. Nelson

Be funny on a golf course?
Do I kid my best friend's mother about her heart condition?

—Phil Silvers

If I died . . . I couldn't play golf.
No way was I giving up golf, so I gave up drinking.
—Bob Hope

The hardest shot is a mashie at ninety yards from the green,
where the ball has to be played against an oak tree, bounces back into
a sandtrap, hits a stone, bounces on the green and then rolls into a cup.
That shot is so difficult I have only made it once.
—Zeppo Marx

**Johnny Carson plays fantastic golf on television
when he stands in front of the camera with
his funny little swing. On the golf course, the man
has trouble walking against the wind.**
—Don Rickles

**Anyone who likes golf on television would
enjoy watching the grass grow on the greens.**
—Andy Rooney

I was attracted to this [television] show for the same reason I'm attracted
to golf: the high degree of difficulty and the endless hope for improvement.
—Glenn Frey

I played Civil War golf:
I went out in 61 and came back in 65.
—Henny Youngman

What do I like about golf? It's certainly not the low scores.
—Huey Lewis

I don't have to tell you what my handicap
is—you told me when I tried to join your club.
—Flip Wilson

My handicap is that I am a one-eyed Negro.
—Sammy Davis, Jr.

I can't hit a ball more than two hundred yards.
I have no butt.
You need a butt if you're going to hit a golf ball.
—Dennis Quaid

A TRUE SWINGER

One of the best-known celebrity golfers of his day, American singer and actor Bing Crosby developed his love of the game and trademark smooth swing as a caddy at the Spokane Country Club, in his home state of Washington. Later, as a member of Lakeside Country Club in the Toluca Lake section of Los Angeles, he played a two handicap and was club champion five times. Crosby was such a golf fanatic that he belonged to nineteen country clubs around the world, and lived in a house overlooking another club in Los Angeles. When that club wouldn't admit him because he was an entertainer, he moved north to Pebble Beach, where the Bing Crosby National Pro-Am was played beginning in 1947.

Crosby lampooned his golfing image in many of his films; in his classic role as Father O'Malley in *Going My Way*, a fellow priest played by Barry Fitzgerald denounces golf (saying "A golf course is nothing but a poolroom moved outdoors"), before Crosby's character teaches him the pleasures of the game. Crosby suffered a fatal heart attack while playing on a golf course outside Madrid in 1977, three years too early to see his son Nathanial become U.S. Amateur Champion.

Crosby once said, "Gentlemen play golf. And if you aren't a gentleman when you start, after the crushing events of the game, you surely become one."

On one hole I'm like Arnold Palmer, and on the next like Lilli Palmer.
—Sean Connery

You've heard of Arnie's Army. Well, those are Dean's Drunks.
—Dean Martin

The ball is man's most disastrous invention, not excluding the wheel.
—Robert Morley

Charley [Pride] hits some good woods—most of them are trees.
—Glen Campbell

Golf has taught me there is a connection between pleasure and pain. "Golf" spelled backwards is "flog."
—Phyllis Diller

One minute it's fear and loathing, but hit a couple of good shots and you're on top of the world. I've gone crazy over this game.
—Jack Nicholson

I couldn't tell you exactly what I like about golf.
Just when you think you've got it mastered, it lets you know you haven't.
I'm just crazy enough to do it.
—Clint Eastwood

**I used golf as a zen exercise . . . I learned
that a person who is able to concentrate
and focus can do almost anything.**
—T. Bone Burnette

There is a certain romance in futility pursued.
A golfer always loses on the golf course.
—Efrem Zimbalist

**It's a faithless love,
but you hit four good shots and
you've started your day right.**
—Dinah Shore

CHAPTER FOURTEEN

THE CADDIES

The golfer is the modern knight-errant, with his faithful esquire,

the caddie, to bear his wooden-headed and iron-headed weapons.

—Gustav Kobbe

The word "caddie" (or "caddy," either spelling is correct) is a legacy of the first ruling female monarch to play the game, Mary Queen of Scots. She was reared in France, where the word *cadet* meant—and still means—a young man, and by extension one who carries implements for his elders and betters. When Mary arrived in Scotland to claim the throne she brought a retinue with her, including many such young bearers. When she took up golf a *cadet* (pronounced ca-DAY) would carry her clubs. The Scots appropriated the word to mean any porter who did odd jobs. On the golf course, that could mean a club repairer, ball marker, or greenkeeper, as well as a club carrier. Gradually, the definition narrowed to one who carries golf clubs for another—not necessarily a young man, nor today, even a man at all.

Caddies in Scotland, generally older men who know a great deal about the game and are accomplished players in their own right, can be outspoken and iconoclastic. In Japan and Europe, caddies are frequently women, and not always young. In America, where caddies were traditionally young boys, they are nearly extinct in club play due to the proliferation of golf carts which began in the 1950s. Caddies continue to work for golfers in tournament play, and may include young women, older men, and the offspring of players—the 1997 PGA Champion Davis Love III employs his younger brother Mark as his caddie.

Perhaps the most famous former caddie to become a champion was Francis Ouimet. As a 20-year-old from The Country Club of Brookline, Massachusetts, he was up against the legendary Harry Vardon and another favored English professional, Ted Ray, in a three-way playoff for the 1913 U.S. Open championship. At the tee, Ouimet's own caddie, a ten-year-old boy named Eddie Lowery, offered Ouimet his driver and the advice, "Keep your eye on the ball, sir." Francis did just that, and became only the second American ever to win a

U.S. Open—though the first was another ex-caddie, Johnny McDermott, from Philadelphia, who won in 1911 and 1912.

At its best, the relationship between a player and his or her caddie is a partnership; Walter Hagen, when he won his first British Open, endorsed the entire prize check over to his caddie. At its worst, the caddie is intrusive and debilitating, a hazard with two legs; the great Spanish champion Seve Ballesteros advises his caddies, "When I make a bad shot, your job is to take the blame."

In the end, a caddie's value is relative to the quality of the player he or she carries for, as comedian Jackie Gleason understood. In the 1950s, New York restaurateur Toots Shor and Honeymooners star Jackie Gleason played a round of golf—during which Shor shot an abominable 211. After a very long day at the course, Shor asked his playing partner, "What should I give the caddie?"

"Your clubs," Gleason responded.

You get either the youngest caddie or the oldest golf cart, and neither works.
—Richard Haskell

Caddies are part valet, part coach, part psychiatrist and mostly invisible.
From behind the gallery ropes, spectators seldom notice them.
Shouldering golf bags big enough to hold supplies for an Arctic expedition,
they trudge in the shadows of their golfers.
—Dave Anderson

Caddies are a breed of their own. If you shoot 66, they say,
"Man, we shot 66!" But go out and shoot 77 and they say, "Hell, he shot 77!"
—Lee Trevino

There were three things in the world that he held
in the smallest esteem: slugs, poets and caddies with hiccups.
—P. G. Wodehouse

There are three rules for a caddy to live by: show up; keep up; shut up.
—Paul Jungman

When I caddied [as a kid in Puerto Rico] I was paid ten cents a bag.
And if you lost a ball, they kicked your butt and fired you. I never lost a ball.
—Chi Chi Rodriguez

**The average caddie can find five balls
while looking for yours—which he can't find.**
—Robinson Murray

The driving range is the sadistic relief center for golf. Here is where golfers
line up to try to hit some poor unfortunate, locked in a steel cage
built around an old jeep. The guy who picks up balls in this contraption
is usually a former caddie who talked too much about his clients'
indiscretions of scoring. Most golfers feel this punishment is too light.
—Herbert I. Kavet

**I know you can get fined for throwing a club.
What I want to know is if
you can get fined for throwing a caddie.**
—Tommy Bolt

Real golfers, whatever the provocation, never strike a caddie with the driver.
The sand wedge is far more effective.
—Huxtable Pippey

The player may experiment about his swing, his grip, his stance.
It is only when he begins asking his caddie's advice
that he is getting on dangerous ground.
—Sir Walter Simpson

From men who have adopted carrying as a trade,
the golfer is entitled to expect the highest standard of efficiency.
If he carries for you regularly, he ought to know what club
you intend to take, and to give it without being asked.
When you are in doubt about how to play your shot, he ought
to confirm you in the opinion you have formed regarding it.
He must never show the just contempt he has for your game.

—Sir Walter Simpson

When I ask you what club to hit,
look the other way and don't you dare say a word.

—Sam Snead, to his caddie

If a caddie can help you, then you don't know how to play golf.

—Dan Jenkins

If I needed advice from my caddie,
he'd be hitting the shots and I'd be carrying the bag.

—Bobby Jones

I was lying tenth and had a thirty-five foot putt. I whispered over my
shoulder: 'How does this one break?' And my caddie said, 'who cares?'

—Jack Lemmon

THE LANGUAGE
OF CADDIES

An American tourist playing St. Andrews sliced his tee shot out of bounds and immediately hit another ball.

"In our country we call that a mulligan," he told his caddie. "What do you call it over here?"

"A three," the caddie replied.

THE CONNUBIAL CADDIE

Doug Mochrie, husband and caddie:

I never swore in my whole life until I met her.

Dottie Mochrie, wife and professional player:

That's a damn lie.

I don't know why that putt hung on the edge.
I'm a clean liver. It must be my caddie.
—JoAnne Carner

A caddie, as a rule, is about as good a caddie
as the disposition of his employer.
—Grantland Rice

I've always had confidence, but Roscoe [Jones]
gave me a double confidence: chemistry.
—Nancy Lopez

I've had the same great wife since 1976, and the same great caddie since 1978.
My caddie, Mike Cowan, certainly knows that my wife is vastly more
important to me than he is, and a whole lot better looking.
That said, however, I also feel I've got the best caddie in the business.
—Peter Jacobsen, just before Cowan defected to Tiger Woods in 1996

We're not the show; the player is. Tiger has taken the world by storm,
and I'm out there with him. He's been wonderful. He is wonderful.
But my life hasn't changed that much. I get a little more attention now, that's all.
—Mike "Fluff" Cowan

Do I every disagree with him on course strategy? Never—unless he's wrong.
—Gary Nicklaus, on caddying for his father Jack

Let's just say that I walk
to a different set of sprinkler heads.

—Greg Ritz, caddie for Curtis Strange and John Daly

There's something haunting about getting up at dawn and walking a golf
course, checking pin placements. It's easy to lose track of reality.

—Ernest "Creamy" Carolan, veteran caddie to Ben Hogan and Arnold Palmer

It was a great honor to be inducted into the Hall of Fame.
I didn't know they had a caddie division.

—Bob Hope

Nobody but you and your caddie care
what you do out there, and if your caddie
is betting against you, he doesn't care either.

—Lee Trevino

My game is so bad I gotta hire three caddies: one to walk
the left rough, one for the right rough, and one down the middle.
And the one in the middle doesn't have much to do.

—Dave Hill

If it wasn't for golf, I'd probably be a caddie today.

—George Archer

CHAPTER FIFTEEN

THE MONEY PLAYERS: GOLF AND BUSINESS

Indeed, the highest pleasure of golf may be that on the fairways and far from all the

pressures of commerce and rationality, we can feel immortal for a few hours.

—Colman McCarthy

Business and golf have formed a natural alliance since the fourteenth century, when the Dutch sold the Scots clubs and balls. But while the British first forged the business-golf alliance, Americans took it to the next level: to expand the franchise, they invented miniature golf, wooden tees, golf-shoe spikes, metal shafts, and driving ranges in the early part of the 20th century. By the 1950s, thanks to television and the riveting post-war rivalry between Ben Hogan and Sam Snead, golf itself became big business. In the next decade, Arnold Palmer and Jack Nicklaus ushered in the age of hefty corporate endorsements.

Today the golfing industry has grown into a $40 billion annual spending spree—not counting side bets on matches. The average American male between the ages of 29 and 43 spends $1,130 each year on green fees and equipment.

Sixty percent of U.S. management plays golf, and being competitive, each works hard at playing well, although the smart executive always manages a poorer game when playing against the boss. Around the world, golf increasingly provides a role model for business, where winning is everything, and a plan of attack, dedication, and learned skills are required to succeed in the global marketplace.

There is even something called an "executive course," which is shorter and therefore faster than a championship course. Ostensibly, executive courses were created so that busy business people could squeeze a quick round of golf into their schedules. But the chief reasons for the growth of executive courses are the enormous increase in the numbers of players and a shortage of suitable land.

High-profile business moguls who play include New York real estate magnate Donald Trump (whose *nom du golf* is "The Trumpster"), with a seven handicap, RJR Nabisco chairman Henry Kravis (nine), and publishing tycoon Nelson Doubleday, financier Charles Schwab and former baseball commissioner Peter Ueberroth, all tied at 11.

Golf is an indispensible adjunct to high civilization.
—Andrew Carnegie

Golf shows an extension of one's personality. If a person is aggressive
on the golf course, he or she will be aggressive in business.
—T. Boone Pickens

The seasoned golfing salesman knows when to win, when to come out all
even, and when to fall apart at the seams and absorb a valuable thrashing.
—Herbert Warren Wind

Never try to do business with someone who is having a bad game.
—William H. Davis

The golf links lie so near the mill
That almost every day
The laboring children
Can look out and watch
The men at play
—Sarah Norcliffe Cleghorn

No other game (lest it be polo) is as thoroughly associated
with capitalism and its oppression as golf.
—John Updike

Golf is typical capitalist lunacy.

—George Bernard Shaw

If you break 100, watch your golf. If you break 80, watch your business.

—Joey Adams

You must never forget that golf is supposed to be a game of relaxation:
it should take your mind off your work, your mortgage, your income tax,
and introduce fresh and much more serious problems into your life.

—Stephen Baker

My worst addiction is golf.
I have a titanium plate in my leg—it's my fifteenth club.

—Lew Rudin, whose leg was crushed when he was run over by a friend's golf cart

Statistics indicate that, as a result of overwork, modern executives are dropping like flies on the nation's golf courses.

—Ira Wallach

I can tell right away if a guy is a winner or a loser
just by the way he conducts himself on the course.

—Donald Trump

I find it more satisfying to be a bad player at golf.
The worse you play, the better you remember the occasional good shot.
—Nubar Gulbenkian

I'm a vice president in charge of special marketing. That means I play golf and go to cocktail parties. I'm pretty good at my job.
—Mickey Mantle

[AFL-CIO President] George Meany plays golf just
like a union man: he negotiates the final score.
—Bob Hope

My worst day on the golf course still beats my best day at the office.
—John Hallisey

I'd play every day if I could. It's cheaper than a shrink
and there are no telephones on my golf cart.
—Brent Musberger

THE PRICE OF GOLF

Even for the wealthiest, the quest for a perfect round of golf on an idyllic, well-manicured course can have tremendous costs—financial and psychological—as David Komansky, CEO of Merrill Lynch explains:

"I joined an expensive country club. I took lessons. I bought the most expensive clubs I could find. I bought every piece of golf gear and clothing you can imagine. I went to Arizona twice for personal lessons from famed golf guru Jim Flick. So, I would estimate that 50 or 60 thousand dollars later here I am. Everyone tells me golf is a fun game. Painful is a more appropriate description. You do see some beautiful places. And I do think it's a great way to spend quality time with clients. But nothing can prepare you for the humbling experience of trying to hit that little white ball."

Your financial cost can be figured out when you realize
that if you were to devote the same time and energy to business instead
of golf, you would be a millionaire in approximately six weeks.
—Buddy Hackett

Give me a millionaire with a bad backswing
and I can have a very pleasant afternoon.
—George Low, Sr.

If I have any genius at all, it must be a genius for play!
I love to play—I love fishing and hunting and trapshooting and
ping-pong and chess and pool and billiards and driving a motor-car,
and at times I love golf, when I can get the shots going
somewhere near right. It seems I love almost any pursuit except work.
—Bobby Jones

**I don't think of myself as a celebrity or superstar.
I'm just an ordinary guy who makes
his living in a crazy way. . . . My only fear is that
I may have to go out and get a real job.**
—Fuzzy Zoeller

I cannot find a job that pays me $700,000 a year, so, until I do, I'll be right here.
—Pat Bradley

I owe everything to golf. Where else could a guy with an IQ like mine make this much money?

—Hubert Green

Because we dress well on the course, people think we're all millionaires.
The truth is that there is less money in pro golf than
in any well-known sport. Out of 144 guys here, at least one hundred
are extremely concerned about their next check.

—Ed Sneed

How would you like to meet the top 143 people at what you do each week in order to survive?

—Bruce Crampton

In a major championship you don't care about the money.
You're just trying to get your name on a piece of silver.

—Nick Faldo

I like the thought of playing for money instead of silverware; I never did like to polish.

—Patty Sheehan, on turning professional

The life of a professional golfer is precarious at best.
Win, and they carry you to the clubhouse on their shoulders.
Lose, and you pay the caddies in the dark.
—Gene Sarazen

I'd probably be the fat lady in a circus right now if it hadn't been for golf.
It kept me on the course and out of the refrigerator.
—Kathy Whitworth

The only reason I ever played golf in the first place
was so I could afford to hunt and fish.
—Sam Snead

Retire to what? I'm a golfer and a fisherman. I've got no place to retire to.
—Julius Boros

My wife said to me the other day, "My God, you may
get to 65 without ever working a day in your life."
—John Brodie, on joining the Senior Tour

If this wasn't my living,
I wouldn't do this if you paid me.

—Christy O'Connor, Jr., after getting rained out

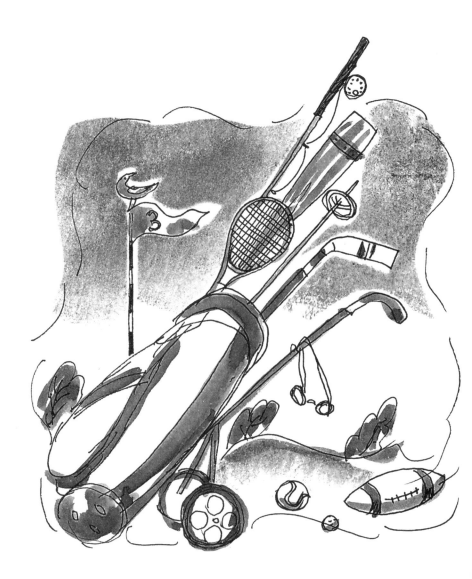

CHAPTER SIXTEEN

THE ATHLETIC GOLFER

Because golf exposes the flaws of the human swing—a basically simple maneuver—it causes more self-torture than any game short of Russian roulette.
—Grantland Rice

As children, athletically inclined girls and boys tend to play at every sport that comes their way. Of necessity, professional athletes must largely confine themselves to the one sport they do best, with the recent exceptions of multi-sport professionals such as Bo Jackson and Deion Sanders, and Michael Jordan's brief foray into baseball notwithstanding. Even serious tennis and swimming may hamper the muscles or discipline of the pro's sport of choice. Golf is the one exception, perhaps because it is not a sport but a game, requiring few muscles and a kind of universal discipline.

Many baseball greats, including Hall of Famers Babe Ruth, Ted Williams, Joe DiMaggio, Mickey Mantle, Ernie Banks, and Johnny Bench, as well as slugger George Brett, home-run king Mark McGwire, and pitcher Orel Hershiser, have taken up golf. The diamond skills do not always translate: as Sam Snead once told Ted Williams, "when we hit a foul ball we have to get out there and play it." Although Johnny Bench plays at scratch, Hershiser to a four handicap, and Brett at a respectable 11, the great DiMaggio is mired at 25.

Football players who also have conquered golf include quarterbacks Mark Rypien and John Elway, with two handicaps, and Joe Namath, with an eight. The most high-profile celebrity athlete golfer, basketball's Michael Jordan, plays at a highly respectable six, while Charles Barkley plays at eight.

Any game where a man sixty can beat a man thirty ain't no game.
—Burt Shotten

You can't call it a sport. You don't run, jump, you don't shoot, you don't pass.
All you have to do is buy some clothes that don't match.
—Steve Sax

I'm definitely not a pioneer.
That's for people like Jackie Robinson and Lee Elder.
I'm just a product of their hard work.
—Tiger Woods

Earl Woods has said a lot of things I don't think bear mention or acknowledge-
ment. Tiger Woods, of course, is a great athlete. I take that back. You don't
have to be a great athlete to play golf. He's a great competitor, and his ability
to focus is tremendous. I put it right there with Michael Jordan and myself.
—Michael Johnson, Olympic 200 meter champion, responding
to Earl Woods's claim that if his son had become a runner, he'd have beaten Johnson

I've never understood people who claim that you don't have to be
a good athlete to be a good golfer. Golf takes patience, hand-eye coordination,
concentration, good nerves, and a fair amount of strength.
A person with all of these qualities would surely get my vote as an athlete.
—Amy Alcott

Golfers are the greatest worriers in the world
of sports. . . . In fast-action sports,
like football, baseball, basketball or tennis,
there is little time to worry compared to the time
a golfer has on his hands between shots.
—Billy Casper

To be able to steady one's play by calling on reserve force is,
as every player knows, the hardest thing to do in any sport.
—Beatrix Hoyt

Golf isn't like other sports where you can
take a player out if he's having a bad day.
You have to play the whole game.
—Phil Blackmar

Who plays golf anymore? I've gone in for gambling now.
At the tables, I only lose my money. On the course, I lose my mind.
—Jackie Miles

THE NATURAL

Mildred Ella Didrikson Zaharias was called "Babe" after Babe Ruth because she regularly hit home runs for her Beaumont, Texas sandlot baseball teams, once hitting five homers in one game. A tomboy who could beat up every boy in her neighborhood, she could also play tennis, polo, soccer, lacrosse, basketball, marbles, billiards, gin rummy—and the harmonica. Babe was an accomplished adagio and ballroom dancer, a roller skater, a diver, and a good cook and seamstress. And she could type one hundred words a minute. She was a one-girl track team: broad jumping, high jumping, putting the shot, throwing the javelin and discus, running the hurdles, and, of course, throwing the baseball.

In college, Didrikson was an All-American girls' basketball player from 1930 to 1932. In that year's combined National Women's A.A.U. track meet and Olympic try-outs she entered eight of the ten events and won five of them, setting three world records. Because women were limited to three events in the 1932 Los Angeles Olympics, Babe entered the 80-meter hurdles, the javelin throw, and the high jump, winning gold medals in the first two. She came relatively late to golf, at the age of 21, and went on to become the greatest woman golfer of her generation, perhaps ever. She dominated the early LPGA tour in the 1940s and 50s, and changed women's golf forever. The first American to win the British women's title, she won three U.S. Women's Open championships and countless other tournaments.

When sportswriter Paul Gallico asked Babe if there was anything she did not play, she replied: "Yeah, dolls."

TILLY SHAFER

The first professional "cross-over" athlete was Arthur J. (Tilly) Shafer, who played baseball for manager John J. McGraw's fabled New York Giants from 1909–1913. He started as a third baseman and was famous for his speed. In 274 professional games he batted .273 and played in two World Series for the Giants, against the Boston Red Sox in 1912 and the Philadelphia Athletics in 1913. During the latter series, he played shortstop and center field in addition to third base, and broke the speed record from third to home when he was timed at 3.1 seconds. Grantland Rice, the legendary sports writer, was ready to crown Shafer King of the Shortstops in an age of great players at the position, including the fading Honus Wagner and Rabbit Maranville: "He is the fastest of the lot—the fastest infielder in the game . . . a better hitter than any of them now, save Wagner, and a better base runner than any rival in sight."

But although he was a natural player, Shafer disliked professional baseball; as a well-bred college man (which is why his teammates called him Tilly), he was toiling way beneath his station in rough-and-tumble times.

To return for another season Shafer demanded a $25,000 salary, an unheard of sum then, and McGraw was willing to offer "only" $20,000. McGraw, who did more to humor Shafer than he did any other player, also made the unprecedented promise that Tilly (who had switched to batting left, improving his average) would never have to bat against a left-handed pitcher! Shafer refused McGraw's offer and went home to Los Angeles to become a successful businessman and to take up golf. Quitting at the zenith of his baseball career, Shafer remained a national hero, but became avid in his new, more socially acceptable sport. Although college graduates never turned pro golfers in those days, Shafer achieved a two handicap, a low score of 69, and three club championships. He played in six California State Amateurs and in the U.S. Amateur in 1929.

Of his second sporting passion, Shafer said, "Golf is a more scientific game than baseball, because it is more delicate and calls for infinitely more concentration. Execution in golf is limited to a fraction of an inch, while in baseball the limits are far greater."

When I hit a ball,
I want someone else to go chase it.
—Rogers Hornsby

The only thing I never learned from [New York Yankees manager]
Billy Martin was how to knock a guy out in the bar.
—JoAnne Carner

I think golf is good for boxing,
but the reverse is far from being the case.
—Max Baer

I played mixed doubles with a whole new foursome yesterday
and I explained that golf was really my game. Of course,
I told my golfing foursome today that tennis was really my game.
—Dinah Shore

Grass? Give me a bucket of balls
and a sand wedge. Sure I like grass.
—Ivan Lendl, who prefers clay courts for his tennis game

Golf is a game of space, and America is a spacious land. . . . This largeness
of scale, the epic earthworks that carve a winding green
firmament beneath a firmament of cloudy blue, is one of the powerful
charms that strikes a newcomer to golf, and that continues
to entrance the duffer heavy with years. The tennis court is a cage
by comparison, and the football field a mirthless gridiron.
—John Updike

In a team sport, you can go out and make your own breaks.
You can make a tackle. You can jump up and block Julius Erving's shot.
Sometimes it's hard. I can't go out and jump on Jack Nicklaus's back.
—Andy North

It's a lot easier hitting a quarterback
than a little white ball.
—Bubba Smith

It took me seventeen years to get three thousand hits in baseball.
I did it in one afternoon on the golf course.
—Hank Aaron

My best golf score is 103,
but I've only been playing fifteen years.
—Alex Karras

I'd rather go to the Super Bowl than shoot 70,
but I'd rather shoot 65 than play in the Super Bowl.
—Lawrence Taylor

I was three over: one over a house, one over a patio
and one over a swimming pool.
—George Brett

He who has fastest golf cart never has a bad lie.
—Mickey Mantle

THE ATHLETIC GOLFER

Baseball reveals character; golf exposes it.
—Ernie Banks

I would rather face the best pitcher that ever lived than be called upon to make a three-foot putt at the critical point of a golf match.
—A. C. "Cap" Anson

It's so ridiculous to see a golfer with a one-foot
putt and everybody is saying "sshh"
and not moving a muscle. Then we allow
19-year-old kids to face a game-deciding
free throw with 17,000 people yelling.
—Al McGuire

Davis Love III turned me on to golf when we were
at North Carolina by showing me it wasn't a sissy game.
—Michael Jordan

The worst thing about getting fired by the [Philadelphia Seventy-] Sixers was
having enough time to work on my golf game—and finding out how bad it was.
—Doug Moe

CHAPTER SEVENTEEN

THE POWER GAME:
KINGS, PREMIERS, AND PRESIDENTS

Golf is a game kings and presidents play when they get tired of running countries.
—Charles Price

Polo may be known as the "Sport of Kings," but reigning monarchs from James IV of Scotland to Edward VIII of the United Kingdom of Great Britain and Northern Ireland (who became the Duke of Windsor after abdicating) have been keen golfers. British Prime Ministers Arthur Balfour and David Lloyd George were also outspoken advocates of the game.

William McKinley was the first American president to enjoy the game, playing a few rounds in 1899 while recuperating from an illness at White Sulphur Springs, West Virginia. Since then, a dozen U.S. presidents from William Howard Taft to Bill Clinton have dabbled (or worse) in golf, and the game has become a part of American political history and the presidential mystique.

Woodrow Wilson was playing golf when the *Lusitania* sank in 1915, drawing the U.S. closer to World War I. Wilson's successor, Warren G. Harding, was among the presidents who played avidly but not particularly well. When he presented the 1921 U.S. Open trophy to Jim Barnes at Columbia Country Club, in Chevy Chase, Maryland with Mrs. Harding and Mrs. Coolidge in attendance, the reluctant 29th President of the United States said, "I'd give anything to be in your shoes today."

In the 1950s, Dwight David Eisenhower probably did more than any other president to popularize the game, and he made no apologies for his 18 handicap and chronic slice. His every game was covered by the press and television. "Ike" installed his "Little White House" on the grounds of Augusta National, home of the Masters Tournament, and added a three-hole putting green on the front lawn of the White House itself.

A more recent Republican duffer was President George Bush, whose aides described his fast-paced, erratic rounds of golf—which often took less than two hours to play—as "cart polo." ("I don't play for scores," he explained, "I like to play fast.") Bush was at least a third-generation golfer. His maternal grandfather and namesake, George Herbert Walker, was a USGA president who gave his name to the Walker Cup—the biannual team contest between the best British and American amateur golfers—and donated the handsome silver trophy that goes to the winning team.

America's current leader, President Clinton, has a 16 handicap, which edges ex-President Gerald Ford (17), and beats George Bush (20) as handily on the course as he did in the electoral college in 1992.

Golf is a game where the ball lies poorly and the player well.
—John Garland Pollard

The difference between golf and government is that in golf you can't improve your lie.
—George Deukmejian

Politics, like music and golf, is best learned at an early age.
—Lawrence Welk

Rail-splitting produced an unparalleled president in Abraham Lincoln, but golf hasn't produced even a good A-1 congressman.
—Will Rogers

If I had my way, no man guilty of golf would be eligible for any office of trust or profit in the United States.
—H. L. Mencken

It does look like a very good exercise. But I wonder what is the little white ball for?
—Ulysses S. Grant, after watching a beginning golfer swing several times without making contact

A tolerable day, a tolerable green, a tolerable opponent ought
to supply all that any reasonably constituted human being should require
in the way of entertainment. The golfer should find no difficulty
in dismissing all worries from his mind and regarding golf, even if it be
indifferent golf, as the true and adequate end of man's existence. Care may
sit behind the horseman, she never presumes to walk with the caddie.
—Lord Arthur J. Balfour

Golf is the only game where the worst player gets the best of it.
He obtains more out of it as regards both exercise and enjoyment,
for the good player gets worried over the slightest mistake,
whereas the poor player makes too many mistakes to worry over them.
—David Lloyd George

There is no reason . . . why golf should not be begun
as soon as one can walk and continued as long as one can walk.
—Lord Arthur J. Balfour

Golf is to me what his Sabine farm was to Horace—a solace and an inspiration.
—Ramsay Macdonald

You get to know more of the character of a man
in a round of golf than in six months of political experience.
—David Lloyd George

Golf always makes me so damned angry.
—King George V of England

Here Eddie, hold the flag while I putt out.
—Walter Hagen to the Prince of Wales (later King Edward VIII)

I like going there for golf. America's one vast golf course today.
—Edward, Duke of Windsor (formerly King Edward VIII), in the 1950s

Golf seems to me an arduous way to go for a walk.
I prefer to take the dogs out.
—Princess Anne of England

Playing golf is like chasing a quinine pill around a cow pasture.
—Winston Churchill

Playing the game I have learned the meaning of humility.
It has given me an understanding of the futility of human effort.
—Abba Eban

Some of us worship in churches,
some in synagogues, some on golf courses.
—Adlai E. Stevenson II

A PRESIDENTIAL PASTIME

William Howard Taft was the first sitting president to play golf seriously, if not all that well. In fact, he had been president of the Cincinnati Country Club, prior to being the 27th President of the United States. During his term in Washington, the 300-pound Taft played golf almost every day, always in striped morning trousers, often at Maryland's Chevy Chase Club, and usually with Todd Lincoln, President Lincoln's eldest son. Explaining his passion for the game, Taft once wrote, "Golf is in the interest of good health and good manners. It promotes self-restraint and . . . affords a chance to play the man and act the gentleman."

Theodore Roosevelt, Taft's predecessor who was famous for his rugged masculinity, had taken up the sport only after he left the White House—while president he played tennis and hunted. Alarmed by the publicity surrounding Taft's chosen recreation, he wrote to his successor: "Photographs of me on horseback, yes, tennis, no. And golf is fatal."

I did not see the sense in chasing a little white ball around a field.
—Calvin Coolidge

When you are in any contest, you should work
as if there were—to the very last minute—a chance to lose it.
This is battle, this is politics, this is anything.
—Dwight D. Eisenhower

President Eisenhower has given up golf for painting. It takes fewer strokes.
—Bob Hope

Augusta is the course Ike Eisenhower usually plays on.
That's proof enough for me that he is a man with good taste.
—Jimmy Demaret

Golf obviously provides one of our best forms of healthful exercise accompanied by good fellowship and companionship.
—Dwight D. Eisenhower

It is true that my predecessor did not object, as I do,
to pictures of one's golf skill in action. But neither,
on the other hand, did he ever bean a Secret Serviceman.
—John F. Kennedy

One lesson you'd better learn if you want to be in politics is that
you never go out on a golf course and beat the President.
—Lyndon B. Johnson

By the time you get dressed, drive out there,
play eighteen holes and come home, you've blown seven hours.
There are better things you can do with your time.
—Richard M. Nixon

I know I'm getting better at golf because I'm hitting fewer spectators.
—Gerald R. Ford

There are 326 golf course in the greater Palm Springs area, and Jerry Ford never knows which one he's playing until after he's teed off.
—Bob Hope

Bob [Hope] says I have made golf a combat and contact sport.
—Gerald R. Ford

If I swung the gavel like I swung a golf club,
the nation would be in a hell of a mess.
—Thomas P. (Tip) O'Neill, while he was Speaker of the U.S. House of Representatives

The problem with golf is I have to deal with a humiliation factor.
—George H. W. Bush

He'd rather face Congress than a three-foot putt.
—Ken Raynor, professional at the Kennebunkport, Maine club where Bush played while in office

In golf, you keep your head down and follow through. In the vice presidency,
you keep your head up and follow through. It's a big difference.
—Dan Quayle

Dan would rather play golf than have sex any day.
—Marilyn Quayle

[Bill Clinton] told me he caddied in the same group with me in the Hot Springs
[Arkansas] Open. That's why I voted for him, because he was my caddie.
—Tommy Bolt

Vice President Al Gore said we have a Tiger Woods economy.
If so, we also have a Frank Gifford military
commanded by a Rodney Dangerfield president.
—Argus Hamilton

Whoa! Mama, stay up.
—Bill Clinton to his ball after teeing off at Martha's Vineyard

OUR DUFFER-IN-CHIEF

President Bill Clinton, a southpaw, is avid enough to play golf right-handed. Unlike President Eisenhower, his putting green at the White House has only one hole, but it was designed by Robert Trent Jones Jr. at a cost of $23,000. Clinton famously injured his left knee during a visit to Greg Norman's house for a golfing break.

Clinton once publicly declared that "people of all ages and walks of life should have the opportunity to compete on the best golf courses the country has to offer." When asked if this would mean that the hoi-polloi would be invited to use the White House putting green, Mike McCurry, President Clinton's press secretary, was quick to put the administration's spin on things: "The problem is that someone will accuse us of charging fifty thou to play."

CHAPTER EIGHTEEN

ON THE GREEN

The game would be nothing without this troublesome business 'round the hole.
—Joyce Wethered (Lady Heathcoat-Amory)

Some paradoxes: 1.) Forty percent of all golf shots are taken on the green, regardless of a golfer's handicap, but 95 percent of all practice time is devoted to the showier driving range, usually with only a few perfunctory last-minute passes at the putting green. 2.) Golfers will blame themselves—or their opponents, the weather, or karma—for bad drives and balls lost in the rough, but they will blame their putters for a bad putt. 3.) Champions who excelled in putting, such as Billy Casper, winner of two U.S. Opens and a Masters, and Arthur D'Arcy (Bobby) Locke, winner of four British Opens and the first successful non-American on the PGA Tour, are step-children in the annals of golf, far less lionized than their long-driving bretheren—even though all agree that it's the short game that wins tournaments. 4.) Despite the second-class citizenship of putts and putters, most post-mortems (and the worst lies) at the 19th hole are about putts.

The grandest irony of all is that the word "putt" comes simply from the word "put"—as in putting the ball into the hole (there being no truth to the assertion that "putt" comes from "puttering," as in wasting time). How to commit such a simple act with the stroke of a club is *the* big mystery of golf. And no one has ever sunk a putt longer than four feet to win the U.S. Open—knowing that he had to make that putt for the championship. Yet the scene of all this agony, the green, is known in golfer's slang as "the dance floor."

Bernhard Langer, the German professional who won the Masters in 1985 and 1993, is the slowest putter in professional golf, averaging 90 seconds per putt—or 50 minutes in a 36-hole tournament—according to a calculation by *Golf* magazine. "I've seen turtles move faster than Bernhard," snapped Lanny Wadkins, one of the faster tour players. The fastest putter on the tour is—big surprise; it's a good thing you're sitting down—John Daly, who averages only 20 seconds per putt.

Putting greens are to golf courses what faces are to portraits.
—Charles Blair MacDonald

Fifty percent of the fairways we play on today are better than ninety percent of the greens we played thirty years ago.
—Jim Ferrier

You drive for show and putt for dough.
—Bobby Locke

There's no need to tell one who has played a great deal of championship golf that it's the short game that decides the contests.
—Tommy Armour

A good player who is a great putter is a match for any golfer. A great hitter who cannot putt is a match for no one.
—Ben Sayers

Those who cannot drive suppose themselves to be good putters.
—Sir Walter Simpson

Putting is really a game within a game.

—Tom Watson

Putting isn't golf. Greens should be treated the same as water hazards:
You land on them, then add two strokes to your score.

—Chi Chi Rodriguez

I would like to knock it on every green
and two-putt, but that's not
my style of play or my style of living.

—Muffin Spencer-Devlin

Hitting a golf ball and putting having nothing in common.
They're two different games. You work all your life to perfect a repeating
swing that will get you to the greens, and then you have to try
to do something that is totally unrelated. There shouldn't be any cups,
just flag sticks. And then the man who hit the most fairways
and greens and got closest to the pins would be the tournament winner.

—Ben Hogan

I enjoy the "oohs" and "aahs" from the gallery
when I hit my drives, but I'm pretty tired
of the "awws" and "uhhs" when I miss the putts.
—John Daly

Putting is the department of golf which, more than any other,
lends itself to experimentation and the exploitation of pet theories.
—Harry Vardon

Putting is like wisdom—partly a natural gift
and partly the accumulation of experience.
—Arnold Palmer

Many golfers enjoy putting to such an extent
that they take three or four putts to the green.
—Grantland Rice

Bad putting is due more to the effect
the green has upon the player
than it has upon the action of the ball.
—Bobby Jones

THE YIPS

The greatest fear of every golfer is the dreaded disease of "the yips," severe cases of nerves accompanied by muscle tension and spasms while attempting to putt. Sam Snead described it as "a disease of the nervous system that strikes any golfer who plays in tournament competition long enough." The yips have humbled even the greatest of golfers—both Ben Hogan and Peter Alliss retired from competition when they could no longer consistently sink short putts.

From switching to oversized "broom handle" putters, to changing to a cross-handed grip on the club or seeing a sports psychologist, most players evolve their game to deal with the problem. Of course perhaps what is most needed is a positive attitude; as Lee Trevino has said, "The ball's got to stop somewhere; it might as well be at the bottom of the hole."

**These greens are so fast I have to hold my putter
over the ball and hit it with the shadow.**
—Sam Snead

Do not allow yourself to be annoyed because your opponent
insists on making elaborate study of all his putts.
—Horace G. Hutchinson

Reading a green is like reading the small type in a contract.
If you don't read them with painstaking care, you are likely to be in trouble.
—Claude Hamilton

The way I putted, I must have been reading the greens
in Spanish and putting them in English.
—Homero Blancas

Long putts travel on the wings of chance.
—Bernard Darwin

Prayer never seems to work for me on the golf course.
I think this has something to do with my being a terrible putter.
—Rev. Billy Graham

That putt was so good, I could feel the baby applaud.
—Donna Horton-White, upon sinking a long putt while seven months pregnant

**It was one of those days you dream about:
every hole seemed to be six inches wide.**
—Tom Purtzer

Putts get real difficult the day they pass the money out.
—Lee Trevino

**I swear I'm the queen of the lip-out.
The ball comes out and looks at me and grins
as if to say, "Too bad; you missed again."**
—Pat Bradley

Those longish second putts take a lot
out of you even when you make 'em.
—Cary Middlecoff

Short putts are missed because it is not physically possible
to make the little ball travel over uncertain ground
for three or four feet with any degree of regularity.
—Walter Hagen

[Walter] Hagen said that no one remembers who finished second.
But they still ask me if I ever think about that putt
I missed to win the 1970 [British] Open at St. Andrews. I tell them
that it sometimes doesn't cross my mind for a full five minutes.
—Doug Sanders

There is nothing so demoralizing
as missing a short putt.
—Bobby Jones

When a putter is waiting his turn to hole out a putt
of one or two feet in length, on which the match hangs on the last hole,
it is of vital importance to think of nothing.
—Sir Walter Simpson

Putting affects the nerves more than anything.
I would actually get nauseated over three-footers, and there were
tournaments when I couldn't keep a meal down for four days.
—Byron Nelson

When I putt, my emotions collide like tectonic plates.
It's left my memory circuits full of scars that won't heal.
—Mac O'Grady

**The devoted golfer is an anguished soul who
has learned a lot about putting just as an avalanche
victim has learned a lot about snow.**
—Dan Jenkins

Gimme: An agreement between two losers who can't putt.
—Jim Bishop

My personal opinion is that more men are good putters from practice
than because they have any pronounced superiority,
to begin with, over other men.
—Francis Ouimet

You can always recover from a bad drive,
but there's no recovering from a bad putt.
It's missing those six-inchers
that causes us to break up our sticks.
—Jimmy Demaret

Never break your putter and your driver
in the same round or you're dead.
—Tommy Bolt

Even when times were good, I realized that
my earning power as a golf professional
depended on too many ifs and putts.
—Gene Sarazen

The trouble with golf is
you're only as good as your last putt.
—Doug Sanders

CHAPTER NINETEEN

AT THE CLUBHOUSE

"N is for nineteenth, the hole that's the best
And the reason some golfers play all of the rest."
—Richard Armour

Talking about the game, usually over a longish cocktail hour, often can seem more important than actually playing it. While any business dealing is done on the course itself, the "19th hole" bar is where the details are nailed down and the agreement celebrated—and in case a friendly wager's been made, it's also where the bets are paid up.

In 1888, one of the first golf courses in America, the St. Andrews Golf Club of Yonkers, New York, consisted of nine holes in an abandoned orchard. The founders met under a large apple tree upon whose branches they hung their outer clothing while playing golf. A table under the tree holding a tub of ice and a pail of water was the country's first 19th hole. The club became known informally as "The Apple Tree Gang." In 1891, Shinnecock Hills Country Club, in Southampton, Long Island, was the first golf club to be chartered in the U.S., and was also the first club in America to build a clubhouse specifically in conjunction with a golf course—and therefore the first place in the country to host other post-game diversions.

Table games are a frequent extension of the 19th hole: dominoes, dice, poker, and gin rummy are the games of choice in most clubs, and bridge is the country club game for those who don't play golf. In English tradition, a simple dice game often determines who buys the post-round drinks, although in America it's usually the day's high scorer, while in Scotland it's the winner. Of course, the real action at the clubhouse is mulling over the day's round—to share in the moments of post-match camaraderie the wonderful mystery of why we love to play this bewitching and bedeviling game called golf.

I like to say I was born on the 19th hole, the only one I ever parred.
—George Low, Jr.

Golf should never be talked about in a sitting position.
The lecturer, in order to gain maximum effectiveness, should act out his stories.
—Stephen Baker

Golf is the hardest game in the world.
There's no way you can ever get it.
Just when you think you do,
the game jumps up and puts you in your place.
—Ben Crenshaw

One reason golf is such an exasperating game is that a thing
we learned is so easily forgotten, and we find ourselves struggling year
after year with faults we had discovered and corrected time and again.
—Bobby Jones

If there is one thing I have learned during my years as a professional,
it is that the only thing constant about golf is its inconstancy.
—Jack Nicklaus

This game is like a horse: if you take your eye off it, it'll jump back and kick your shins for you.

—Byron Nelson

One of the most fascinating things about golf is how it reflects the cycle of life. No matter what you shoot, the next day you have to go back to the first tee and begin all over again and make yourself into something.

—Peter Jacobsen

Like life, golf can be humbling. However, little good comes from brooding about mistakes we've made. The next shot, in golf or in life, is the big one.

—Grantland Rice

They say golf is like life, but don't believe them. Golf is more complicated than that.

—Gardner Dickinson

I didn't need to finish college to know what golf was all about. All you need to know is to hit the ball, find it and hit it again until it disappears into the hole in the ground.

—Fuzzy Zoeller

Experts who have studied the matter assure us that the mind
can only think of one thing at a time. Obviously, they have never made
a study of golfers, or they would lower their estimate.
—Robinson Murray

Golf is a game where guts, stick-to-it-iveness and blind devotion
will always net you absolutely nothing but an ulcer.
—Tommy Bolt

Golf is an ideal diversion, but a ruinous disease.
—B. C. Forbes

My goal is to play 72 holes someday without changing expression.
—Jack Renner

Nothing has changed since caveman days when some Neanderthal
in plaid pants first picked up a club and tried to groove an inside-out path.
We're all still looking for a repeating swing that works.
—Glen Waggoner

The traditions of the game are rich with memories of dramatic triumphs as well
as heartbreaking failures. The best players fail the most because they are
in the hunt all the time. You learn to handle it—accept it or you don't survive.
—Deane Beman

**Golf is a game in which perfection
stays just out of reach.**
—Betsey Rawls

No one has ever conquered this game.
One week out there and you are God;
next time you are the devil.
—Juli Inkster

**I never knew what top golf was like until
I turned professional. Then it was too late.**
—Steve Melnyk

Golf was never meant to be an exact science—it's an art form.
Einstein was a great scientist but a lousy golfer.
—Bob Toski

**Golf is not, on the whole, a game for realists.
By its exactitudes of measurement
it invites the attention of perfectionists.**
—Heywood Hale Broun

Golf is not a game of great shots. It's a game of the most misses.
The people who win make the smallest mistakes.
—Gene Littler

No man has mastered golf until he realizes that his good shots are accidents and his bad shots good exercise.
—Eugene R. Black

I love to sweat and heave and breathe and hurt and burn
and get dirty. . . . There's something good about getting all dirty
and grimy and nasty and then showering: you feel twice as clean.
—Jan Stephenson

The biggest liar in the world is the golfer who claims
that he plays the game merely for exercise.
—Tommy Bolt

A golfer might as well turn in his clubs if he can't find some excuse for his own duffery.
—Milton Gross

You can't alibi a 100 score down to 80.
—Don Herold

May you live long enough to shoot your age.
—Traditional English golf toast

Golf keeps the heart young and the eyes clear.
—Andra Kirkady

Golf is a puzzle without an answer. I've played golf
for forty years and I still haven't the slightest idea how to play.
—Gary Player

Few learn golf in a lifetime.
—Grantland Rice

We all mature . . . and gain experience from golf and travel
and life in general. When you look back at some of the things you
said or but it's all part of the learning curve. If you screw up,
you screw up. Nobody ever put an arm around my shoulder
and guided me through the minefield.
—Nick Faldo

I realize that there are no guarantees in this game—not to mention
in this life—and we have only a short time to enjoy it.
—Scott Simpson

Never hurry, never worry, and always
remember to smell the flowers along the way.
—Walter Hagen

Play each shot as if it's the first shot you're ever going to play.
The tournament starts on the next shot you hit.
—Greg Norman

No way. Golf's too boring.
—Morgan-Leigh Norman, Greg's daughter,
when asked if she would take up her father's game

It is almost impossible to remember how tragic a place the world is when one is playing golf.
—Robert Lynd

When I look on my life and try to decide out of what I have
got the most pleasure, I have no doubt at all in
saying that I have got more out of golf than anything else.
—Lord Brabazon

You know you're getting old when you start watching golf on TV and enjoying it.
—Larry Miller

I'm not a golfaholic; I did my golfaholic period.
—Johnny Miller, on becoming eligible for the Senior Tour at age 50

I've been getting pumped up for the Open and similar championships
for 42 years. . . . I suppose when the day comes that I'm not excited
and I don't have some rumblings in my stomach, I won't play . . . but somewhere
in my makeup and thinking there might be a chance I could win again.
—Arnold Palmer

I have loved playing the game and practicing it. Whether my schedule
for the following day called for a tournament round
or merely a trip to the practice tee, the prospect that there was going
to be golf in it made me feel privileged and extremely happy.
I couldn't wait for the sun to come up so that I could get out on the course again.
—Ben Hogan

You'll never get anywhere fooling around those golf courses.

—Clara Hogan, to her son, Ben, when he was 16

Few things draw two men together more surely than a mutual inability
to master golf, coupled with an intense and ever-increasing love of the game.

—P. G. Wodehouse

Golf is the equivalent of crack for middle-aged white men.

—Mike Barnicle

It's no longer nerdy to play golf.

—James Paleno, golf coach at Pacific Palisades High School in suburban Los Angeles

Golf actually makes for international understanding, drawing men together
as it does through their common sorrows. The standard alibis have
been freely translated into every known language, including bad language.

—Robinson Murray

Golf and sex are about the only things
you can enjoy without being good at them.

—Jimmy Demaret

Golf is like sex. If you don't take it seriously it's no fun.
If you do take it seriously, it breaks your heart.
—Arnold Daly

Golf is a fickle game and must be wooed to be won.
—William Park, Jr.

The fun you get from golf is in direct ratio to the effort you don't put into it.
—Bob Allen

Golf is like love.
One day you think you're too old,
and the next you can't wait to do it again.
—Roberto DeVincenzo

Golf is the most fun you can have without taking your clothes off.
—Chi Chi Rodriguez

Golf is the cruelest of sports. Like life, it's unfair. It's a harlot, a trollop.
It leads you on. It never lives up to its promises.
It's not a sport, it's bondage. An obsession. A boulevard of broken dreams.
It plays with men. And runs off with the butcher.
—Jim Murray

Golf is neither a microcosm of nor
a metaphor for Life. It is a sport,
a bloodless sport if you don't count ulcers.
—Dick Schaap

There is no shape, no size of body, no awkwardness nor
ungainliness which puts good golf beyond reach.
There are good golfers with spectacles, with one eye, with one leg,
even with one arm. In golf, while there is life there is hope.
—Sir Walter Simpson

Every great golfer has learned to think positively,
to assume the success and not the failure of a shot, to disregard misfortune
and to accept disaster, and never to indulge the futility
of remorse and blame. These are the hardest lessons of all.
—Pat Ward-Thomas

It is nothing new or original to say that
golf is played one stroke at a time.
But it took me many years to realize it.
—Bobby Jones

BIOGRAPHICAL INDEX OF QUOTATIONS